ROUND ONE

or Vienna in the 1890s

a Schnitzler Variation

Eric Bentley

BROADWAY PLAY PUBLISHING INC
224 E 62nd St, NY, NY 10065
www.broadwayplaypub.com
info@broadwayplaypub.com

ROUND ONE
© Copyright 1954, 1982, 2008, by Eric Bentley

First printing: December 2008
I S B N: 0-88145-409-5

Book design: Marie Donovan
Word processing: Microsoft Word
Typographic controls: Ventura Publisher
Typeface: Palatino
Printed and bound in the U S A

ROUND TWO/ROUND ONE

ROUND ONE, in its day, provoked what was possibly
the biggest theater scandal ever. Here is what we find in
the *Deutsch-Österreichische Tages-Zeitung*, Vienna, April
24, 1922:

"Lust for money and power were always the driving
force of all Jewish transactions. Productions of REIGEN
have for a long time now been much more than a
business: they are a test of power through which Jewry
(Juda) wishes to show that in this age-old cultural
center of the German spirit it has taken to itself the
power."

To whom then did Vienna belong—Arthur Schnitzler
or the Nazis? Sigmund Freud or Adolf Hitler? In 1938
the former fled to a quiet death in London while the
latter entered Vienna in a triumphal march.

Of course productions of REIGEN were never a test of
political or social power but the anti-semites should be
thanked for finding more in REIGEN than anyone else
did. Read properly, it does pack a punch. And it does
speak for a sophisticated sense of civilization that no
fanatic of any persuasion can accept. That REIGEN
shocks puritans is the least of it—and the worst of it.
The *Tages-Zeitung* just cited provided the standard
puritanic putdown: "The aim is not the satisfaction of
artistic needs but the exploitation of the easily-aroused
erotic feelings." Note here the double error: it is
assumed, first, that a work should not arouse erotic

feelings and, second, that Schnitzler's purpose was precisely to arouse such feelings. The truth could not be more different. Though in principle Schnitzler would not have objected to open eroticism ("arousing erotic feelings") REIGEN happens to be a comedy, and comedy is apt to make fun of such feelings. Schnitzler has even replaced the sexual act, in this play, with asterisks on his page or a blackout on his stage. (Oskar Straus, at one point, composed a pleasant Viennese waltz to be played during this blackout.) REIGEN is indeed so serious a comedy that over-serious readers, especially medical men, have found in it a warning against "promiscuity" and unprotected sex in a time of rampant syphilis. (Winston Churchill's father was one of its many victims.) I might add that when I wrote Round Two in the nineteen eighties, one serious reader said my characters seemed to him to be passing AIDS along...

What is it that the characters in ROUND ONE actually do? Each of them, as we say, "has sex" with two partners and makes no full or sincere commitment to either one. To the *Tages-Zeitung* that was both disgusting and titillating—a terrifying mix. To some critics, scholars and physicians it was dangerous to the health and much needed the exposure which, they felt, Schnitzler's play gave it. Two schools of thought, or pseudo-thought, are here at odds with each other. One sees ROUND ONE as the enemy in the great war of the age, Aryans versus Semites. The other sees it as a potential friend and ally in the current war against syphilis. Both take any production of the play as an urgent socio-political act, if not an act *of* war, at least an act *in* a war.

How wrong they both were! For this play is not propaganda of any sort, it is not even didactic. That its author, a medical man himself, must, in 1900, have been acutely aware of the dangers of syphilis is true but such awareness is not present in Reigen, and the notion that he may be warning a future generation against AIDS is absurd. As to the proto-Nazi attack in the *Tageszeitung*, Schnitzler might have seen that coming, but it has not influenced the text of his play. And when it came, and other troubles followed, Schnitzler did not return the fire of the "Nazis". He withdrew the play from stages all over Europe: performances were not to be licensed for the duration of his copyright. Thus REIGEN had no presence on the European stage until 1982.

The American stage is a different matter, for the United States had very different copyright laws. This part of the REIGEN story begins in 1950 with a film of which the title was a French translation of the word "Reigen": "La Ronde". Initially, the film was banned by the New York authorities, not indeed as semitic, but as indecent. It was a Jewish attorney that took the case all the way to the Supreme Court and won, if much to the consternation of Roman Catholic officials who saw in REIGEN as great a threat to social stability as the Viennese Nazis had.

The film was shown, at least in art houses, all over the United States. Did this mean that Schnitzler's work could at last emerge as what it was, a work of art, a comedy, by a worthy contemporary of Shaw and Wilde? It had high credentials, a cast of first rank French actors, and a director of great talent and taste, Max Ophuls . But from here on I must cease to tell the story from the outside and "objectively" because I was on the inside, and a subjectivity.

I reviewed the Ophuls film in *The New Republic*. Unfavorably. For though indeed this film was a breakthrough of sorts, presenting REIGEN as a work of art, and not as any kind of propaganda or didacticism, I found it untrue to the original, not in the spirit of the author. Schnitzler abhorred the myth of Gay Vienna ("gay" in its traditional, not its sexual, meaning), the frivolous Vienna of Strauss waltzes in which the Danube is a mythical blue, its actual color in Viennese territory, a dull brown. But Ophuls' film hewed all too closely to that stereotype. It was, in every sense, too light. Which fact enabled it to get by the Supreme Court but prevented it bringing Schnitzler's clinical realism and rawness to the American public.

At this time, I was in touch with Schnitzler's son Heinrich who was Arthur's heir and handled theatrical rights. On the Ophuls film, his opinion was the same as mine or perhaps I should say my opinion was the same as his as he had been lecturing me about Arthur's disbelief in Gay Vienna for years. But when I proposed to make a new translation of the play which would be authentic Schnitzler he did not want it to be produced but stood by his father's express wish that it be withheld from all theaters. I would have respected Arthur's wishes except that I learned at this time that the German text was not protected by U S copyright law. I must therefore assume that if I did not offer a translation to a theater someone else would. Arthur's wishes, in any case, had not become a stipulation in his will, and I didn't feel I had the same obligation to respect them as had his son and heir.

The rest is history. I made the translation and offered it to the outstanding Off Broadway theater of the time, Circle in the Square, "the Square" being Sheridan Square, where it was produced by Theodore Mann and Jose Quintero. Quintero's 1955 direction of REIGEN was not only a correction of the Ophuls film, it was, in North America at least, the first production of the play as a work of art , not more, not less, a story the moving images of which define ten human beings, and this not to titillate or enflame an audience, nor on the other

hand to teach them to use safe sex, but to amuse and
entertain them (this comedy *is* a comedy) and to
present a Schnitzlerian vision of things: in the midst
of life we are in death, but in the midst of death we are
in life. Our audiences at Circle in the Square left the
theater rather sadly, I thought, though much of the time
during the actual performance they were smiling
broadly or even laughing loudly. And I found myself
asking total strangers, what has this play done for you,
what would you say is its point, if any, what does it
add up to, if anything? Not all the responses I got
were single words, or even one liners. Some had to
be provided *in extenso* in a neighboring bar. Let me
attempt to extract the essence of the more interesting
replies:

First off, the form of REIGEN, the famous daisy chain,
is paradoxical: the play is centered, yet not centered,
in the sexual act. This is the play all about fucking,
which is the play about anything but fucking: the
sexual act is off stage and thus unseen, while drama
consists of what you see on stage. So is Schnitzler
playing a game with us? By all means: was not a
B B C-T V Schnitzler series entitled Games of Love
and Death? Death may not be prominent in REIGEN
but is present in the shadows and notably in the first
scene and the last. Both the Soldier who starts the play
and the Count who finishes it are close companions of
the Grim Reaper. What is more prominent in the play is
of course Love, that is, the idea or hope (or despair) of
Love. Love is on everyone's tongue but has not reached
anyone's heart.

The form of REIGEN—A in bed with B, B with C,
C with D etcetera—calls so much attention to itself that
people, including professional critics, have had trouble
seeing anything else and thus, in the press, we have
often found REIGEN described as hardly a play at all.

Did not Schnitzler himself regard it as but a series
of conversations? In a letter, he even suggested it had
no great literary pretension. The conversations are
structured, of course, being neatly arranged in twos,
the first leading to orgasm, the second away from
orgasm. Which might give Schnitzler a sound claim
to originality in playwriting except that critics who
know their history will say No, this dual structure
is simply a derivation from two Hogarth paintings
entitled "Before" and "After".

Myself, I am inclined to concede that these paintings
may indeed have been Schnitzler's starting point. But
they are not more than that. Hogarth portrays a single,
if presumably typical, seduction. On his canvases we
catch two moments in the process and find out nothing
more about the two people involved, let alone about
a third, fourth, or fifth person in that environment.
In REIGEN we are confronted with ten distinct human
beings in a continuing action, with something more
than hints of their past and their future. At a first
reading or viewing, it may be that only the repetitions
of this "plot" are noticed but a second and third will
reveal more and more. One may note, for example, that
while each character has two partners, he (or she) does
not have two similar partners, nor yet two partners
neatly contrasted with each other. In a character's first
encounter, you will find the seed of his (or her) second.:
the reason why he or she needs or at least seeks a
different kind of partner, the differences all set forth
in the dialogues. The way the upper-class Husband,
for instance, talks to his Young Wife in his first scene
prepares us for his choice of partner in his second
scene: it will be a Viennese type known as The Little
Miss, a working class girl who will not take money
from the man who picks her up but will gladly give
him sex in return for dinner and drinks in a good
restaurant... And such a forward thrust also works

backwards: in a character's second scene, you also
recognize the different mask he or she wore in the
first scene.

So you are making a mistake if you view REIGEN as
a succession of asterisks or blackouts which signify a
succession of orgasms, but you are no closer to the full
truth of the matter if you view it as a circle or carousel
(i.e. movement in a circle), though of course this
metaphor is alive within the play. If the structure
were indeed circular, one would, at the end, be back
at the beginning. But one is not. The play opens with
the encounter of Whore and Soldier. The latter is the
crudest character in the play, a man who has almost
totally given up his humanity. Other people exist just
to provide him with a physical release. Thus in the
interplay of body and soul which is the life of this play
and the characters in it, he stands at one extreme, and
the Count in the last scene stands at the other. The
Count is so intent on proving that the soul is more real
than the body that he actually forgets he has had sex
with the whore and fantasizes about a conceivable
relation, even with a whore (!), that is "romantic", i.e.
spiritual. Thus REIGEN has what most commentators
seem to have denied it: a development of plot and
theme from one extremity to another.

And what gives this development its justification, its
energy and its point? It is a variation or serious parody
of a standard pattern: the development of sinners from
their fleshly sins and commitments upwards toward
heaven and all things spiritual. Shades of Wagner's
Tannhäuser and a thousand lesser works! For the
spirituality of the Count, though well meant, is not
authentic. He thinks he hasn't "had sex", but he has.
And when he realizes this, he can only regret that
reality is less attractive than illusion and look forward
to his next talk with his philosophical friend Lulu

(Louis) who perhaps can find a form of words that will perform a miracle...

As to the Before and After pattern, every scene except the last (which presents the After but not the Before) does conform to it, and thus if sexual intercourse were the goal, all the characters could be deemed successful, even the Count whose intercourse is forgotten. But very evidently, intercourse was not the goal, and none of them feel successful, except possibly the Soldier of scene one who in a cynicism that betokens despair has abandoned not only all hope of happiness but even the dream of it. All the others do dream of it, and speak of love as what would produce happiness. Love in what sense? Love mostly undefined and vague, as befits a dream. Through orgasm to love—that is one underlying formula—the hope that, through orgasm, one might arrive at love. One can of course hope for love with a less pretentious aim in view: simple intimacy. And what the people of Vienna and REIGEN *are* seeking in all those beds is intimacy. Only the Soldier is incapable of it. The others achieve it in different degrees and styles. Even the Whore can manage a degree of it when she has a civilized partner like the Count.

"Only connect" —famous formula of E M Forster. Sexual intercourse thinks of itself as the ultimate connection. Parental coition gave birth to all of us, so we feel entitled to expect *some* benefit from almost any bedroom encounter. We get to be disappointed. What can be the most intimate and loving connection is often, perhaps usually, and in Vienna 1900 always, loveless and even if very exciting ("that was terrific sex!") spiritually empty, leaving the coupling couple strangely and negatively affected. Conversations following sex (of which Schnitzler has here provided ten examples) defines the "degrees of separation" between the parties.

They may think of themselves as sensual, even lecherous, but actually they are people who hope that sensuality, or even a mere pretense of it, and the ability to fuck will end their isolation, their *in*sulation.

They are insulated, yes, each of them marooned on his own little island. Arthur Schnitzler once remarked that the title of one of his other plays would also fit REIGEN. It is *Der einsame Weg*, The Lonely Way.

CHARACTERS & SETTING

The Whore
The Soldier
The Parlor Maid
The Young Gentleman
The Young Wife
The Husband
The Little miss
The Poet
The Actress
The Count

Time: The eighteen-nineties.

Place: Vienna

ROUND ONE is dedicated to the memory of
José Quintero
who gave the American theater its first glimpse of this
play

Wien, Wien, nur Du allein
Sollst stets die Stadt meiner Träume sein...

1
THE WHORE AND THE SOLDIER

(Late in the evening. On the Augarten Bridge)

*(*SOLDIER, *on his way home, whistling)*

WHORE: Hey, Angel Face! Wanna come with me?

SOLDIER: Me? Angel Face?!

WHORE: I live near here.

SOLDIER: Gotta get back to the barracks.

WHORE: It's nicer with me.

SOLDIER: *(Near her now)* Could be.

WHORE: A cop might come!

SOLDIER: I got my sword on.

WHORE: So come with me!

SOLDIER: I got no money.

WHORE: I don't need no money.

*(*SOLDIER *stops. They are under a street lamp.)*

SOLDIER: You don't need no money?

WHORE: A soldier like you can get me for nothing.

SOLDIER: So you're the one Huber told me about....

WHORE: I don't know no Huber.

SOLDIER: The café in the Schiff Gasse. He went home with you.

WHORE: I've taken plenty of guys home from there. Eh! *(Her eyes tell how many.)*

SOLDIER: Let's go then.

WHORE: In a hurry now?

SOLDIER: Gotta be back in the barracks at ten.

WHORE: How long you been in the army?

SOLDIER: No business of yours. Live far from here?

WHORE: Ten minutes' walk.

SOLDIER: Too far. How about a kiss?

(WHORE kisses SOLDIER.)

WHORE: That's the best part. When I like a guy.

SOLDIER: No. I can't go with you.

WHORE: Come tomorrow then. In the afternoon.

SOLDIER: Give me the address.

WHORE: Only—I bet you won't come.

SOLDIER: I will.

WHORE: How about over there? *(She points toward the Danube.)*

SOLDIER: Aw, that's no good.

WHORE: It's always good—with me. How long do we have to live?

SOLDIER: Okay, then. But make it snappy.

(SOLDIER and WHORE walk.)

WHORE: Easy. It's so dark there. One slip, and you're in the Danube.

SOLDIER: Might be the best thing.

WHORE: Pst! Hey, wait. There's a bench.

SOLDIER: You know your way around.

WHORE: Wish I had a guy like you for a boyfriend.

SOLDIER: I'd make you jealous.

WHORE: I could take care of that.

SOLDIER: Think so?

WHORE: Not so loud. Could be a cop around at that—he might've got lost. You wouldn't think we were right in the middle of Vienna, would you?

SOLDIER: Come over here!

WHORE: If we slip, we're in the river!

(SOLDIER *has grabbed hold of* WHORE.)

SOLDIER: Ah! now...

WHORE: Hold on tight.

SOLDIER: Don't worry...

*****

WHORE: It'd have been a lot better on the bench.

SOLDIER: Hm... You gettin' up.

WHORE: Where are you rushing off—

SOLDIER: Got to get back to the barracks. I'm late.

WHORE: What's your name, soldier?

SOLDIER: My name?

WHORE: Mine's—Leocadia.

SOLDIER: That's a new one!

WHORE: Soldier...

SOLDIER: Well, what do you want?

WHORE: How about a dime for the janitor?

SOLDIER: What do you think *I* am? Goodby! Leocadia...

WHORE: You crook! You son of a bitch!

(SOLDIER is gone.)

2
THE SOLDIER AND THE PARLOR MAID

(The Prater. Sunday evening. A path leading from the Wurstelprater—or amusement park—out into dark avenues of trees. The din of the amusement park is audible. So is the sound of the Fünfkreuzertanz—a banal polka—played by a brass band. SOLDIER. PARLOR MAID.)

PARLOR MAID: Why did you keep wanting to leave?

(SOLDIER laughs stupidly; he is embarrassed.)

PARLOR MAID: I thought it was marvelous. I love dancing.

(SOLDIER takes PARLOR MAID by the waist.)

PARLOR MAID: *(Letting him)* But we're not dancing *now.* Why'd you hold me so tight?

SOLDIER: What's your name? Kathi?

PARLOR MAID: You have a Kathi on your mind.

SOLDIER: I've got it: Marie.

PARLOR MAID: It's dark here. I'm scared.

SOLDIER: Nothing to be afraid of with me on hand!

PARLOR MAID: But where are we going? There's no one around. Let's go back. How *dark* it is!

SOLDIER: *(Pulling at his Virginia cigar till the tip glows)* See it get lighter? Ha! My little treasure!

PARLOR MAID: Hey! What are you doing? If I'd known this...

SOLDIER: Nice and soft! Damned if you're not the nicest and softest in the whole bunch, *Fräulein!*

PARLOR MAID: What whole bunch?

SOLDIER: In there.

PARLOR MAID: You tried all of them?

SOLDIER: You see a lot of things. Dancing.

PARLOR MAID: You danced with that blonde more than with me. The one with the face.

SOLDIER: Friend of a buddy of mine.

PARLOR MAID: The corporal with the turned-up mustache?

SOLDIER: Nah. The civilian. The one at the table with me before. With the hoarse voice?

PARLOR MAID: Oh, yes. He's pretty fresh.

SOLDIER: Did *he* try something with you?

PARLOR MAID: I just saw how he was with the other girls.

SOLDIER: Now, *Fräulein*, tell me...

PARLOR MAID: Ooh! You'll burn me with that cigar.

SOLDIER: Oh, pardon me, *Fräulein*—or can I call you...Marie?

PARLOR MAID: We haven't known each other very long.

SOLDIER: Hell, there's lots of people use first names and don't even like each other.

PARLOR MAID: Let's make it next time, when... You see, Herr Franz...

SOLDIER: You got my name!

PARLOR MAID: You see, Herr Franz...

SOLDIER: Make it just—Franz, *Fräulein*.

PARLOR MAID: *You* mustn't be so fresh. Sh! What if somebody comes!

SOLDIER: What if they do? You can't see six feet in front of you. *(Still walking)*

PARLOR MAID: But, heavens, where are we getting to?

SOLDIER: Look! There's two just like us.

PARLOR MAID: Where? I can't see a thing.

SOLDIER: There!

PARLOR MAID: Why do you say like *us*?

SOLDIER: Oh, I mean—they kinda like each other.

PARLOR MAID: Hey, watch out! What was that? I nearly fell.

SOLDIER: It's these railings round the grass.

PARLOR MAID: Don't push so hard. I'll fall over.

SOLDIER: Sh! Not so loud!

PARLOR MAID: Look now I'm *really* going to scream! What are you doing...hey...

SOLDIER: There's no one for miles around.

PARLOR MAID: Let's go back with the rest of them.

SOLDIER: But we don't need *them*, Marie, what we need is...uh, huh...

PARLOR MAID: Herr Franz, please! For Heaven's sake!! Now listen, if I'd had...any idea...oh! ...Oh!! ...Yes...

*****

SOLDIER: *(Blissfully)*. Jesus Christ Almighty! ...Ah-h!...

PARLOR MAID: ...I can't see your face.

SOLDIER: My face? ...Hell!

*****

SOLDIER: Now look, *Frulein*, you can't stay in the grass all night.

PARLOR MAID: Oh, come on, Franz, help me up!

SOLDIER: Okay. *(He grabs her.)* Oops!

PARLOR MAID: You're a bad man, Franz. *(Walks away)*

SOLDIER: Oh, so that's it? Hey, wait for me!

PARLOR MAID: What did you let me go for?

SOLDIER: Can't I get this cigar lit for God's sake?

PARLOR MAID: It's so dark.

SOLDIER: Well, tomorrow it'll be light.

PARLOR MAID: Tell me something—do you like me?

SOLDIER: I thought you noticed!

(SOLDIER laughs. They walk.)

PARLOR MAID: Where are we going?

SOLDIER: Why, back!

PARLOR MAID: Oh, please, Franz, not so quick!

SOLDIER: What's wrong? I don't like running around in the dark.

PARLOR MAID: Tell me, Franz, do you...like me?

SOLDIER: I just told you I liked you.

PARLOR MAID: Then, give me a little kiss.

SOLDIER: *(Condescending)* Here...listen! You can hear that music now.

PARLOR MAID: You want to go dancing again?

SOLDIER: Sure. What's wrong with that?

PARLOR MAID: Well, Franz, look, I must be getting back. They'll gripe anyhow, the lady of the house is such a... she'd like it best if we *never* went out!

SOLDIER: Sure. You go home then.

PARLOR MAID: Herr Franz! I thought...you might take me.

SOLDIER: Home?

PARLOR MAID: Oh, please, it's so dreary—going home alone!

SOLDIER: Where do you live?

PARLOR MAID: It's not far—Porzellan Gasse.

SOLDIER: Oh! Then we go the same way.... But it's too early for me! I want some fun. I got a late pass tonight. Don't have to be back in the barracks till twelve. I'm going dancing.

PARLOR MAID: *I* see how it is. It's that blonde. The one with the face.

SOLDIER: Her face ain't so bad.

PARLOR MAID: You men are wicked! I bet you do this with every girl.

SOLDIER: That might be too many.

PARLOR MAID: Franz, do me a favor. Not tonight— stay with me tonight, look...

SOLDIER: Okay, okay. But I can dance for a while first, I suppose?

PARLOR MAID: Tonight I'm not dancing with anyone but you.

SOLDIER: Here's the dance hall. And they're still playing *that* thing. *(He sings with the band.)* ...All right, if you wanna wait, I'll take you home. If not, I'll say good night.

PARLOR MAID: I think I'll wait.

SOLDIER: Get yourself a beer. *(Turning to a blonde, dancing by with her boy, putting on a "refined" accent.)* May I have the pleasure?

3
THE PARLOR MAID AND THE YOUNG GENTLEMAN

(A hot summer afternoon. His parents are off in the country. The cook is having her half-day. In the kitchen, PARLOR MAID *is writing* SOLDIER *a letter; he is her lover. There is a ring from* YOUNG GENTLEMAN'*s room. She gets up and goes into the room.* YOUNG GENTLEMAN *is lying on the sofa with cigarette and French novel.)*

PARLOR MAID: You rang, Herr Alfred?

YOUNG GENTLEMAN: Oh, yes...Marie... yes, I did ring as a matter of fact.... Now what was it? ...Oh, I know, let the blinds down, Marie, will you? ...It's cooler with the blinds down...don't you think?...

*(*PARLOR MAID *goes to the window and lets the Venetian blinds down.)*

YOUNG GENTLEMAN: *(Going on reading)* What are you doing, Marie? That's right. Oh, but now I can't see to read.

PARLOR MAID: The way you always study so, Herr Alfred!

YOUNG GENTLEMAN: *(Passing over this loftily)* That'll be all, thanks.

*(*PARLOR MAID *goes out.)*

*(*YOUNG GENTLEMAN *tries to go on reading; soon lets the book fall; rings again.)*

*(*PARLOR MAID *is in the doorway.)*

YOUNG GENTLEMAN: Look, Marie...now, um, what I was going to say...well...yes, is there any cognac in the house?

PARLOR MAID: Yes, Herr Alfred. But it's locked up.

YOUNG GENTLEMAN: Oh. Who has the key?

PARLOR MAID: Lini.

YOUNG GENTLEMAN: Lini?

PARLOR MAID: The cook, Herr Alfred.

YOUNG GENTLEMAN: Oh. Then go and tell Lini.

PARLOR MAID: Lini's having her half-day.

YOUNG GENTLEMAN: Oh.

PARLOR MAID: Shall I run over to the café, Herr Alfred?

YOUNG GENTLEMAN: Oh, no...I don't need cognac anyway. Listen, Marie, bring me a glass of water. Wait, Marie—let it run, hm? Till it's quite cold?

(PARLOR MAID goes.)

(YOUNG GENTLEMAN is watching her go when PARLOR MAID turns round at the door. He stares into space. She turns the faucet on and lets the water run. Meanwhile, she goes to her little room, washes her hands, and arranges her curls in the mirror. Then she brings him the glass of water. She walks to the sofa.)

(YOUNG GENTLEMAN raises himself part way. PARLOR MAID puts the glass in his hand. Their fingers touch.)

YOUNG GENTLEMAN: Oh. Thanks... Well, what is it? Now be careful. Put the glass back on the tray.... *(He lies back and stretches out.)* What's the time?

PARLOR MAID: Five o'clock, Herr Alfred.

YOUNG GENTLEMAN: I see. Five. Thank You.

(PARLOR MAID goes; at the door, she turns; YOUNG GENTLEMAN is looking; she notices and smiles.)

(YOUNG GENTLEMAN *lies where he is for a while, then suddenly gets up. He walks to the door; then returns and lies down on the sofa. He tries to read again. Fails. Again rings)*

(PARLOR MAID *enters with a smile which she makes no attempt to hide.)*

YOUNG GENTLEMAN: Look, Marie, what I was going to ask you...didn't Doctor Schueller stop by this morning?

PARLOR MAID: No.

YOUNG GENTLEMAN: Well. That's strange. You know Doctor Schueller?

PARLOR MAID: The tall gentleman with the big black beard?

YOUNG GENTLEMAN: Yes. Maybe he *did* call?

PARLOR MAID: No one called, Herr Alfred.

YOUNG GENTLEMAN: *(Taking the plunge)* Come here, Marie.

PARLOR MAID: *(Coming a little closer)* Yes, Herr Alfred?

YOUNG GENTLEMAN: Closer...yes...um...I only thought...

PARLOR MAID: Yes, Herr Alfred?

YOUNG GENTLEMAN: About that blouse, what kind is it? ...Oh, come closer, I won't bite.

PARLOR MAID: *(Comes)* You don't like my blouse, Herr Alfred?

(YOUNG GENTLEMAN *takes hold of the blouse and, in so doing, pulls* PARLOR MAID *down on him.)*

YOUNG GENTLEMAN: Blue, is it? Yes, what a lovely blue! You're very nicely dressed, Marie.

PARLOR MAID: Oh, Herr Alfred!

YOUNG GENTLEMAN: Well, you are! *(He's opened the blouse. Matter-of-fact)* You've got lovely white skin, Marie.

PARLOR MAID: You're flattering me, Herr Alfred.

YOUNG GENTLEMAN: *(Kissing her bosom)* Does this hurt?

PARLOR MAID: Oh no!

YOUNG GENTLEMAN: Why do you sigh like that?

PARLOR MAID: Oh, Herr Alfred...

YOUNG GENTLEMAN: And what nice slippers you have on...

PARLOR MAID: ...but...Herr Alfred...if the doorbell rings...

YOUNG GENTLEMAN: Who'd ring at this hour?

PARLOR MAID: But, Herr Alfred...you see, it's so light!

YOUNG GENTLEMAN: Oho, you needn't be embarrassed with me! You needn't be embarrassed with anybody... pretty as you are! You know, your hair has such a pleasant smell.

PARLOR MAID: Herr Alfred...

YOUNG GENTLEMAN: Don't make such a fuss, Marie. I've *seen* you.... When I came in late the other night, and went for a glass of water, the door to your room was open...and I was...

PARLOR MAID: *(Hides her face)* Heavens, I'd no idea you could be so naughty, Herr Alfred.

YOUNG GENTLEMAN: I saw...this...and this...and this...and...

PARLOR MAID: Herr Alfred!!!!!!

YOUNG GENTLEMAN: Come...here...that's right, yes...

PARLOR MAID: But if anyone rings...

YOUNG GENTLEMAN: Now stop it, for Heaven's sake. We won't go to the door.

*****

(The doorbell rings.)

YOUNG GENTLEMAN: *(Adjusting his clothes)* Christ Almighty! ...What a racket the man makes! Maybe he rang before and we just didn't pay attention.

PARLOR MAID: *(Adjusting her clothes)* Oh, I kept my ears open the whole time.

YOUNG GENTLEMAN: Well, now go and see—through the peephole.

PARLOR MAID: Herr Alfred... You *are*... No! ...A naughty man!

YOUNG GENTLEMAN: Now please, go take a look.

(PARLOR MAID goes. YOUNG GENTLEMAN quickly pulls up the Venetian blinds.)

PARLOR MAID: *(Comes back)* There's no one there. Maybe it *was* Doctor Schueller.

YOUNG GENTLEMAN: *(Disagreeably affected)* That'll be all, thanks.

(PARLOR MAID comes closer.)

YOUNG GENTLEMAN: *(Retreating)* Look, Marie, I'm going. To the café.

PARLOR MAID: *(Tenderly)* So soon...Herr Alfred?

YOUNG GENTLEMAN: *(Severely)* If Doctor Schueller should come...

PARLOR MAID: He won't.

YOUNG GENTLEMAN: *(More severely)*. If Doctor Schueller should come, I...I...I'm—in the café. *(He goes into the next room.)*

(The PARLOR MAID *takes a cigar from the smoking-table, slips it in her pocket, and goes out.)*

4
THE YOUNG GENTLEMAN AND THE YOUNG WIFE

(Evening. A drawing-room in a house in the Schwind Gasse, furnished with cheap elegance.)

*(*YOUNG GENTLEMAN *has just come in and, still in hat and overcoat, lights the candles. He then inspects the adjoining bedroom, takes an atomizer from the dressing table and sprays the pillows with a fine stream of violet perfume. Then he goes with the spray through both rooms, squeezing the little bulb the whole time, so that soon the whole place smells of violets. He takes off hat and overcoat, sits down in a blue velvet arm-chair; gets up to make sure that the green shutters are drawn, then opens a cupboard in the drawing room, takes out a silver tray laden with pastries, a cognac bottle, and two liqueur glasses, and puts it all on the table. Then he pours himself a glass of cognac and quickly drinks it, looks at his watch, paces the room. When he draws the blue curtains screening the door to the bedroom, the doorbell rings. He gives a start, drops into an armchair and only rises when the door opens and* YOUNG WIFE *enters. She stands for a moment with her left hand on her heart, as though she had to master intense emotion. Her face is covered with veils.)*

YOUNG GENTLEMAN: *(Goes to her, takes her left hand, and imprints a kiss on the white, black-trimmed glove; softly)* I thank you.

YOUNG WIFE: Alfred—Alfred!

YOUNG GENTLEMAN: Come in, dear lady...come in, Frau Emma.

YOUNG WIFE: Let me alone for a moment, please—
oh, please, Alfred! *(She stays close by the door.)*

*(*YOUNG GENTLEMAN *stands before* YOUNG WIFE,
holding her hand.)

YOUNG WIFE: Where am I, actually?

YOUNG GENTLEMAN: In my house.

YOUNG WIFE: This place is a horror, Alfred.

YOUNG GENTLEMAN: What? It's very dignified!

YOUNG WIFE: I met two men on the stairs.

YOUNG GENTLEMAN: People you know?

YOUNG WIFE: They may be. I'm not sure.

YOUNG GENTLEMAN: Forgive me—you must know
who you know!

YOUNG WIFE: But I didn't see a thing.

YOUNG GENTLEMAN: Even if they'd been your best
friends, they couldn't have recognized you. Even I...
if I didn't know it was you...this veil...

YOUNG WIFE: There are two.

YOUNG GENTLEMAN: Won't you come a bit farther in?
And anyway do take off your hat.

YOUNG WIFE: What are you thinking of, Alfred? I told
you—five minutes. No, not a second more! I swear...

YOUNG GENTLEMAN: Then the veil!

YOUNG WIFE: There are two.

YOUNG GENTLEMAN: Oh well, both veils—at least I'm
allowed to see you!

YOUNG WIFE: Do you *really* love me, Alfred?

YOUNG GENTLEMAN: *(Deeply hurt)* Emma, can you
ask...?

YOUNG WIFE: It's so hot in here.

YOUNG GENTLEMAN: You still have your fur cape on—you'll catch cold!

YOUNG WIFE: *(At last steps into the room, throwing herself into an armchair)* I'm dead tired.

YOUNG GENTLEMAN: Permit me. *(He takes her veils off, takes out the hatpin, puts hat, pin, and veils down side by side on the sofa.)*

(YOUNG WIFE lets it happen.)

(YOUNG GENTLEMAN stands before her, shaking his head.)

YOUNG WIFE: What's the matter?

YOUNG GENTLEMAN: Never were you so beautiful!

YOUNG WIFE: How's that?

YOUNG GENTLEMAN: Alone...alone with you...Emma...

(YOUNG GENTLEMAN sinks on one knee beside the armchair, takes both YOUNG WIFE hands and covers them with kisses.)

YOUNG WIFE: And now...let me go. I have done what you asked.

(YOUNG GENTLEMAN drops his head on to YOUNG WIFE's lap.)

YOUNG WIFE: You promised to be good.

YOUNG GENTLEMAN: Yes.

YOUNG WIFE: This room's stifling.

YOUNG GENTLEMAN: *(Gets up)* You still have your cape on.

YOUNG WIFE: Put it with my hat.

(YOUNG GENTLEMAN takes off YOUNG WIFE's cape and puts it on the sofa along with the hat and the other things.)

YOUNG WIFE: And now—*adieu*—

YOUNG GENTLEMAN: Emma!

YOUNG WIFE: The five minutes are up.

YOUNG GENTLEMAN: No, no! You haven't been here one minute yet!

YOUNG WIFE: Alfred, please, tell me exactly what time it is.

YOUNG GENTLEMAN: Quarter past six, on the nose.

YOUNG WIFE: I should have been at my sister's long ago.

YOUNG GENTLEMAN: You can see your sister any time....

YOUNG WIFE: Oh God, Alfred, why did you get me to do this?

YOUNG GENTLEMAN: Because I...worship you, Emma.

YOUNG WIFE: How many women have you said that to?

YOUNG GENTLEMAN: Since I saw you, none.

YOUNG WIFE: What a frivolous woman I am! If anyone had told me—a week ago...or even yesterday...

YOUNG GENTLEMAN: It was the day before yesterday you promised...

YOUNG WIFE: Because you kept tormenting me. But I didn't want to, God is my witness—I didn't want to. Yesterday I'd made up my mind.... I even wrote you a long letter last night.

YOUNG GENTLEMAN: I didn't get it.

YOUNG WIFE: I tore it up. I should have sent it!

YOUNG GENTLEMAN: Instead, you—

YOUNG WIFE: It's scandalous of me! I can't understand myself! Good-bye, Alfred, let me go.

(YOUNG GENTLEMAN *takes* YOUNG WIFE *in his arms and covers her face with hot kisses.*)

YOUNG WIFE: So this is...how you keep you promise?

YOUNG GENTLEMAN: One more kiss! Just one.

YOUNG WIFE: The last!

(YOUNG GENTLEMAN *kisses* YOUNG WIFE, *she reciprocates, and their lips stay together.*)

YOUNG GENTLEMAN: Now I know what happiness is.

(YOUNG WIFE *sinks back in an armchair.*)

YOUNG GENTLEMAN: (*Sits on the arm of the chair, putting his arm gently round her neck*) ...Or rather, now I know that happiness *might* be.

(YOUNG WIFE *gives a profound sigh.*)

(YOUNG GENTLEMAN *kisses* YOUNG WIFE *again.*)

YOUNG WIFE: Alfred, Alfred, what are you making of me?

YOUNG GENTLEMAN: It's not really so uncomfortable here, is it? And so much safer than out of doors.

YOUNG WIFE: Don't remind me.

YOUNG GENTLEMAN: Even those meetings in the park I shall think of with delight! Every minute I've spent at your side will linger forever in the memory.

YOUNG WIFE: You remember the Industrial Ball?

YOUNG GENTLEMAN: Do I remember? ...Didn't I sit next to you at supper? The champagne your husband—

(YOUNG WIFE *gives* YOUNG GENTLEMAN *a look of protest.*)

YOUNG GENTLEMAN: I was only going to speak of the champagne! And Emma, wouldn't you like a glass of cognac?

YOUNG WIFE: Maybe just a drop. But first a glass of water.

YOUNG GENTLEMAN: Yes...now, where is... Oh yes. *(He draws the curtains back from the door and goes into the bedroom.)*

(YOUNG WIFE follows him with her eyes.)

(YOUNG GENTLEMAN returns with a filled decanter and two glasses.)

YOUNG WIFE: Where were you?

YOUNG GENTLEMAN: In the—next room.

(YOUNG GENTLEMAN pours a glass of water for YOUNG WIFE.)

YOUNG WIFE: I'm going to ask you something, Alfred, and you must tell the truth.

YOUNG GENTLEMAN: I swear...

YOUNG WIFE: Was there ever another woman in these rooms?

YOUNG GENTLEMAN: Emma, this house has been around for twenty years!

YOUNG WIFE: You know what I mean, Alfred... with you...

YOUNG GENTLEMAN: With me, here? Emma! You couldn't think such a thing!

YOUNG WIFE: Then you have... But no, I'd better not ask you. It's my own fault. We pay for everything!

YOUNG GENTLEMAN: But what is it? *What* do we pay for?

YOUNG WIFE: No, no, no, I mustn't return to consciousness—or I'd sink into the ground for very shame.

YOUNG GENTLEMAN: *(Still with the decanter in his hand, sadly shakes his head)* Emma, if only knew how you hurt me!

*(*YOUNG WIFE *pours herself a glass of cognac.)*

YOUNG GENTLEMAN: I'll tell you something, Emma. If you're ashamed to be here—if I'm nothing to you— if you don't feel that for me you're all the bliss in all the world—then leave. Leave.

YOUNG WIFE: That is just what I'll do.

YOUNG GENTLEMAN: *(Seizing her hand)* But if you realize that I can't live without you, that to kiss your hand means more to me than all the caresses of all the women in the world. Emma, I'm not like the other young men who know how...this sort of thing is done...call me naïve if you wish...I...

YOUNG WIFE: But what if you *were* like the other young men?

YOUNG GENTLEMAN: Then you wouldn't be here now: you aren't like the other young women.

YOUNG WIFE: How do you know?

*(*YOUNG GENTLEMAN *has drawn* YOUNG WIFE *on to the sofa and sits down close beside her.)*

YOUNG GENTLEMAN: I've thought about you. You're unhappy.

*(*YOUNG WIFE *looks pleased.)*

YOUNG GENTLEMAN: Life is so empty, so trivial. And so short.... Isn't life frightfully short, Emma? There is only one happiness: to find someone who loves you.

*(*YOUNG WIFE *has taken a candied pear from the table and puts it into her mouth.)*

YOUNG GENTLEMAN: Give me half! *(She offers it to him with her lips.)*

(YOUNG WIFE *takes the* YOUNG GENTLEMAN'*s hands, which threaten to go astray.*)

YOUNG WIFE: What are you doing, Alfred? Is this your promise?

YOUNG GENTLEMAN: *(Swallows the candied fruit, then says more boldly)* Life is so short!

YOUNG WIFE: *(Feebly)* But that's no reason...

YOUNG GENTLEMAN: Come, come, my only one, my only...

(YOUNG GENTLEMAN *lifts* YOUNG WIFE *off the sofa.*)

YOUNG WIFE: What are you doing?

YOUNG GENTLEMAN: It's not light in *there.*

YOUNG WIFE: Is there another room?

YOUNG GENTLEMAN: *(Taking her with him)* A lovely one...and quite dark.

YOUNG WIFE: I'd rather stay here.

(The YOUNG GENTLEMAN *has already got her through the curtains and into the bedroom; he begins to unhook* YOUNG WIFE'*s dress at the waist.*)

YOUNG WIFE: It *is* dark. You're so... Oh God, what are you doing? ... Alfred!

YOUNG GENTLEMAN: Emma, I worship you!

YOUNG WIFE: Wait, please, at least wait... *(Weakly)* Go, I'll call for you.

YOUNG GENTLEMAN: Let me...let you help me...let... me...help...you...

YOUNG WIFE: But you're tearing everything!

YOUNG GENTLEMAN: Don't you wear a corset?

YOUNG WIFE: Never. The great Eleanora Duse doesn't wear a corset. You can unbutton my boots.

(Young Gentleman unbuttons Young Wife's boots, kisses her feet.)

YOUNG WIFE: *(Slipping into the bed)* Oooh, I'm cold.

YOUNG GENTLEMAN: It'll get warm.

YOUNG WIFE: *(Laughing softly)* You think so, eh?

YOUNG GENTLEMAN: *(Not liking this, to himself).* She shouldn't have said that! *(He undresses.)*

YOUNG WIFE: *(Tenderly)* Come, come, come!

YOUNG GENTLEMAN: *(In a better mood at once)* I come!

YOUNG WIFE: It smells of violets here.

YOUNG GENTLEMAN: It's you...yes... *(Close by her)* ...you.

YOUNG WIFE: Alfred...Alfred!!!!

YOUNG GENTLEMAN: Emma...

*****

(Young Gentleman and Young Wife are under the bedclothes. It is less dark.)

YOUNG GENTLEMAN: I must be too much in love with you...that's why...I'm nearly out of my mind.

YOUNG WIFE: Hm?

YOUNG GENTLEMAN: All these past days I've been going crazy. I felt it coming on.

YOUNG WIFE: Don't worry about it.

YOUNG GENTLEMAN: Of course not, you can almost take it for granted when a man...

YOUNG WIFE: Don't...don't... You're nervous. Just relax...

YOUNG GENTLEMAN: Do you read Stendhal?

YOUNG WIFE: Stand what?

YOUNG GENTLEMAN: There's a story in his book *On Love* that's most significant.

YOUNG WIFE: Yes?

YOUNG GENTLEMAN: A bunch of officers talk about their love affairs. And each one says that with the woman he loved most...most passionately...she made him...with her he...well, the fact is, it happened to every one of them...what happened to me with you just now.

YOUNG WIFE: And anyway...you *promised* to be good.

YOUNG GENTLEMAN: Please don't laugh.

YOUNG WIFE: I'm not laughing. That story's interesting. I'd always thought it happened only with older men... or with very...well, you know, men who've had more *amour* than was good for them.

YOUNG GENTLEMAN: Nonsense! And by the way, I forgot the most charming story in the Stendhal. A lieutenant of hussars says he spent three nights with a woman he'd been wanting for weeks—and they didn't do a thing but cry with happiness—both of them... *(This is taken from* De L'amour, *Chapter 60: "Failures".)*

YOUNG WIFE: *Both* of them?

YOUNG GENTLEMAN: Does that surprise you? I find it so understandable. Specially when you're in love.

YOUNG WIFE: There must be a lot who don't cry.

YOUNG GENTLEMAN: *(Nervously)* Surely...it was an exceptional case.

YOUNG WIFE: Oh...I thought maybe he said all hussars cry on these occasions.

YOUNG GENTLEMAN: There, you're just making fun...

YOUNG WIFE: Not in the least. Don't be so childish, Alfred.

YOUNG GENTLEMAN: I have the feeling you're thinking of it the whole time.

YOUNG WIFE: I'm not!

YOUNG GENTLEMAN: You are. If I could only be sure you love me!

YOUNG WIFE: Come, give me your sweet little head.

(YOUNG GENTLEMAN *does so.*)

YOUNG GENTLEMAN: Oh, this is *good.*

YOUNG WIFE: Do *you* love *me*?

YOUNG GENTLEMAN: I'm so happy!

YOUNG WIFE: But you don't have to cry as well!

YOUNG GENTLEMAN: *(Moves away, highly irritated)* Again, again! Didn't I beg you?

YOUNG WIFE: I only said you shouldn't cry.

YOUNG GENTLEMAN: You said "Cry *as well.*"

YOUNG WIFE: You're nervous, my dear.

YOUNG GENTLEMAN: I know that.

YOUNG WIFE: You shouldn't be. It's rather nice that... that we—that we—we're...just comrades, as you might say...

YOUNG GENTLEMAN: Now you're starting over.

YOUNG WIFE: Don't you remember one of our very first talks: we wanted to be... "just comrades..." Oh, it was lovely that time...at my sister's in January, at the great ball...during the quadrille.... For Heaven's sake, I should have left long ago! My sister will be waiting—what shall I tell her? *Adieu*, Alfred....

YOUNG GENTLEMAN: Emma! Stay another five minutes!

YOUNG WIFE: All right, five minutes. But you must promise to keep quite still... Yes? ...I'm going to give you a good-bye kiss.... Ssh...keep still, as I told you, or I'll get right up and go. My sweet...sweet...

YOUNG GENTLEMAN: Emma...I worsh...

*****

YOUNG WIFE: Darling Alfred...

YOUNG GENTLEMAN: Oh, it's heaven with you!

YOUNG WIFE: But now I really *must* go.

YOUNG GENTLEMAN: Oh, let your sister wait.

YOUNG WIFE: I must go *home*. It's too late for my sister. What time is it now?

YOUNG GENTLEMAN: How'd I find *that* out!

YOUNG WIFE: By looking at your watch!

YOUNG GENTLEMAN: But it's in my waistcoat.

YOUNG WIFE: Well, get it.

YOUNG GENTLEMAN: *(Gets up with a mighty heave. He is naked.)* Eight.

YOUNG WIFE: *(Rising hastily. She is half-naked.)* For Heaven's sake! Quick, Alfred, my stockings— whatever shall I say? They'll be waiting for me....

YOUNG GENTLEMAN: When do I see you next?

YOUNG WIFE: Never.

YOUNG GENTLEMAN: Emma! Don't you still love me?

YOUNG WIFE: That's why. Give me my boots.

YOUNG GENTLEMAN: Never again? ...Here!

(YOUNG GENTLEMAN hands YOUNG WIFE the boots.)

YOUNG WIFE: There's a buttonhook in my pocket book. Please hurry...

YOUNG GENTLEMAN: Here!

(YOUNG GENTLEMAN hands YOUNG WIFE the buttonhook.)

YOUNG WIFE: Alfred, this can cost us both our necks!

YOUNG GENTLEMAN: *(Not liking this at all)* Why?!

YOUNG WIFE: Well, what can I tell him when he asks me where I've been?

YOUNG GENTLEMAN: At your sister's.

YOUNG WIFE: Yes, if only I were a good liar.

YOUNG GENTLEMAN: You'll just have to be.

YOUNG WIFE: All this for a man like you... Let me give you another kiss. *(She embraces him.)* And now leave me alone, go in the other room, I can't dress with you around.

*(*YOUNG GENTLEMAN *goes to the drawing room and gets dressed.)*

YOUNG WIFE: *(Calling out)* Alfred!

YOUNG GENTLEMAN: Yes, my treasure?

YOUNG WIFE: Maybe it's good we didn't just cry.

YOUNG GENTLEMAN: *(Smiles, not without pride)* You're a very naughty girl.

YOUNG WIFE: What will it be like if we meet at a party one day—by chance?

YOUNG GENTLEMAN: One day? By chance? Surely you'll be at the Lobheimers' tomorrow?

YOUNG WIFE: Yes. Will you?

YOUNG GENTLEMAN: Of course. *(He is now dressed.)* May I ask for the cotillion?

YOUNG WIFE: Oh, I won't go. How can you think...? Why... *(She enters the drawing room, fully dressed, and takes a chocolate pastry.)* ...I'd sink into the ground!

YOUNG GENTLEMAN: *(Taking a pastry)* Well, tomorrow at the Lobheimers'. That's lovely.

YOUNG WIFE: No, no, I'll send word I can't come.... Definitely...

YOUNG GENTLEMAN: Then the day after tomorrow— here.

YOUNG WIFE: What an idea!

YOUNG GENTLEMAN: At six.

YOUNG WIFE: There are cabs at the corner, aren't there?

YOUNG GENTLEMAN: As many as you like. Then it's day after tomorrow, six o'clock, here. Say yes, my dearest treasure.

YOUNG WIFE: ...We'll talk it over—tomorrow during the cotillion.

YOUNG GENTLEMAN: *(Embracing her)* Angel!

YOUNG WIFE: Don't spoil my hair-do again.

YOUNG GENTLEMAN: So it's tomorrow at the Lobheimers' and the day after—in my arms.

YOUNG WIFE: Good-bye...

YOUNG GENTLEMAN: *(Suddenly worried again)* What are you going to tell *him* tonight?

YOUNG WIFE: Don't ask...it's too dreadful. Why do I love you so? Good-bye. If I meet people on the stairs I shall have a stroke!

(YOUNG GENTLEMAN kisses YOUNG WIFE's hand yet again.)

(YOUNG WIFE goes.)

YOUNG GENTLEMAN: *(Left alone. He sits down on the sofa. Then he smiles away to himself.)* An affair with a respectable married woman!

5
THE YOUNG WIFE AND THE HUSBAND

(A comfortable bedroom. It is 10:30 at night. YOUNG WIFE *is lying in bed, reading.* HUSBAND *comes into the room in his bathrobe.)*

YOUNG WIFE: *(Without looking up)* You've stopped working?

HUSBAND: Yes. I'm tired. And besides...

YOUNG WIFE: Yes?

HUSBAND: I suddenly felt so lonely at my desk. Began longing for you.

YOUNG WIFE: *(Looks up)* Really?

HUSBAND: *(Sits by her on the bed)* Don't read any more tonight. You'll ruin your eyes.

YOUNG WIFE: *(Closes the book)* What is it?

HUSBAND: Nothing, my child. I'm in love with you. But you know that.

YOUNG WIFE: One might almost forget it sometimes.

HUSBAND: One even *has* to forget it sometimes.

YOUNG WIFE: Why?

HUSBAND: Marriage would be imperfect otherwise. It would—how shall I put it? It would lose its sanctity.

YOUNG WIFE: Oh...

HUSBAND: If in the course of the five years we've been married we hadn't sometimes forgotten we're in love, we probably *wouldn't* be in love right now.

YOUNG WIFE: That's over my head.

HUSBAND: We've had something like ten or twelve different love affairs with one another...isn't that right?

YOUNG WIFE: I haven't kept count.

HUSBAND: If we'd pushed our first affair to the limit, if I'd blindly surrendered myself to my passion for you from the beginning, we'd have gone the way of millions of others. By now we'd be through.

YOUNG WIFE: I see what you mean.

HUSBAND: Believe me—Emma—in the first days of our marriage I was afraid it would turn out that way.

YOUNG WIFE: So was I.

HUSBAND: That's why it's best—from time to time— to live together just as friends.

YOUNG WIFE: Oh, I see.

HUSBAND: That way we can always keep having new honeymoons, because I never risk letting the weeks of the honeymoon...

YOUNG WIFE: ...run into months.

HUSBAND: Exactly.

YOUNG WIFE: And now it seems ... another of those periods of friendship has come to an end?

HUSBAND: *(Tenderly pressing her to him)* It could be so!

YOUNG WIFE: But suppose it was different—with me?

HUSBAND: It isn't different with you. You're the cleverest creature alive—*and* the most bewitching. I'm happy to have found you.

YOUNG WIFE: So you do know how to court a woman— from time to time. I'm glad.

HUSBAND: *(Has got into bed)* To a man who's seen the world a bit—put your head on my shoulder—marriage means something far more mysterious than to girls from good families like you. You come to us pure and—to a certain degree—ignorant, and so you have a clearer view of the true nature of love than we have.

YOUNG WIFE: *(Laughing)* Oh!

HUSBAND: We're insecure—confused by the experiences we have before marriage. You women hear a lot, and know too much, I'm afraid you read too much too, but you never really find out what we men have to go through. What's commonly called love is made utterly repellant to us—because, after all, what *are* the poor creatures we have to resort to?

YOUNG WIFE: Yes, what *are* the poor creatures you have to resort to?

HUSBAND: *(Kisses her on the forehead)* Be glad, my child, that you never had even a glimpse of their condition. Most of them are rather pitiable beings, but let us not cast the first stone!

YOUNG WIFE: You pity them?

HUSBAND: *(With fine mildness)* They deserve our pity! You girls from good families, who quietly wait beneath the parental roof till a decent man proposes to you— you don't know the poverty that drives those poor creatures into the arms of sin.

YOUNG WIFE: They sell themselves?

HUSBAND: I'm not thinking merely of material misery. There is also—one might say—a moral misery: an insufficient grasp of what is...proper, and especially of what is noble.

YOUNG WIFE: Why pity them, though? Don't they have rather a nice time of it?

HUSBAND: These creatures are destined by nature to sink forever lower and lower and lower.

YOUNG WIFE: *(Snuggles up to him)* Sinking sounds rather attractive!

HUSBAND: *(Pained)* How can you say that, Emma? Surely there could be nothing more repellant to a decent woman than the thought of...

YOUNG WIFE: Oh, of course. I said it without thinking. It's so nice when you talk like this. Tell me more about those creatures!

HUSBAND: What an idea!

YOUNG WIFE: Tell me about your youth.

HUSBAND: Why does *that* interest you?

YOUNG WIFE: Aren't you my husband? And I know nothing about your past?

HUSBAND: I hope you don't think I'd... No, Emma! It would be profanation!

YOUNG WIFE: And yet you've...held any number of young ladies in your arms, the way you're holding me now.

HUSBAND: "Ladies!" *They* are not...

YOUNG WIFE: One question you *must* answer. Or else...no honeymoon.

HUSBAND: Remember, my child, you're a mother— our little girl is sleeping in there.

YOUNG WIFE: *(Pressing herself to him)* But I want a boy too.

HUSBAND: Emma!

YOUNG WIFE: Oh, don't be so... Of course I'm your wife, but I'd like to be—your mistress!

HUSBAND: You would?

YOUNG WIFE: First, my question! Was there a—
a married woman—among them?

HUSBAND: *(Somewhat disturbed)* What makes you ask?

YOUNG WIFE: I'd like to know if there...I mean...there
are women like that, I know... But have *you*...

HUSBAND: Is there such a woman among your friends?

YOUNG WIFE: Well, how could I say yes—or no—
and be sure?

HUSBAND: Has one of your women friends... People talk
a lot when they...women among themselves...has one
of them confessed ...?

YOUNG WIFE: *(Uncertainly)* No.

HUSBAND: Do you *suspect* any of your friends...

YOUNG WIFE: Suspect...well...suspect...

HUSBAND: You do!

YOUNG WIFE: Definitely not, Karl! Now I think it over,
I wouldn't believe it of one of them!

HUSBAND: Promise me something, Emma.

YOUNG WIFE: Well?

HUSBAND: Promise me you'll never go around with
a woman if you have the slightest suspicion that...
her life is not beyond reproach.

YOUNG WIFE: You need a promise for that?

HUSBAND: It often happens that women of ill repute
seek the company of respectable women, partly for
contrast and partly out of a certain—how shall I put it?
—out of a certain nostalgia for virtue.

YOUNG WIFE: I see.

HUSBAND: Yes, so very true, what I just said: Nostalgia for virtue! For there's one thing you can be sure of: all these women are very unhappy.

YOUNG WIFE: Why?

HUSBAND: Imagine the existence they have to lead. Full of meanness, lies, treachery—and danger!

YOUNG WIFE: I'm sure you're right.

HUSBAND: Indeed, they pay for that bit of happiness...that bit of...

YOUNG WIFE: ...pleasure.

HUSBAND: Pleasure? What makes you call it pleasure?

YOUNG WIFE: Well, it's something, or they wouldn't do it.

HUSBAND: It's nothing. Mere intoxication.

YOUNG WIFE: (*Thoughtfully*) Mere intoxication.

HUSBAND: Not even! But—it's bought at a price!

YOUNG WIFE: Then...you do know what you're talking about?

HUSBAND: Yes, Emma. It's my saddest memory.

YOUNG WIFE: Was it long ago. Before you married me?

HUSBAND: Don't ask. Please, don't ask.

YOUNG WIFE: But Karl!

HUSBAND: She is dead.

YOUNG WIFE: Honest?

HUSBAND: Yes... It may sound ridiculous, but I have the feeling *all* these women die young.

YOUNG WIFE: Did you love her very much?

HUSBAND: Can a man love a liar?

YOUNG WIFE: Then, why...?

HUSBAND: Intoxication...

YOUNG WIFE: So it *is*...

HUSBAND: Please, don't talk about it. All that is long past. I've only loved one woman: you. A man can only love where he finds purity and truth!

YOUNG WIFE: Karl!

HUSBAND: Oh how safe, how good a man feels in these arms! Why didn't I know you as a child? I'd never have looked at another woman.

YOUNG WIFE: Karl!

HUSBAND: You're beautiful...beautiful... Oh! *(He puts the light out.)*

*****

*(*HUSBAND *and* YOUNG WIFE *are naked but under the bedclothes.)*

YOUNG WIFE: You know what I can't help thinking of tonight?

HUSBAND: What, my treasure?

YOUNG WIFE: Of...of Venice.

HUSBAND: Our first night...

YOUNG WIFE: Yes... Like that...

HUSBAND: What is it? Tell me.

YOUNG WIFE: Tonight...you love me like that.

HUSBAND: Like that.

YOUNG WIFE: Ah...if you could always...

HUSBAND: *(In her arms)* Yes?

YOUNG WIFE: Oh Karl dear!

HUSBAND: What was it you wanted to say? If I could always...?

YOUNG WIFE: Well, yes.

HUSBAND: Well, what would happen if I could always...?

YOUNG WIFE: Then I'd always know you love me.

HUSBAND: Yes. But you know it anyhow. A man can't always be the loving husband, he must, as Schiller says, go out into a hostile world and fight the good fight! Always remember this, my child. In marriage there's a time for everything. There aren't many who still remember their Venice after five years!

YOUNG WIFE: No.

HUSBAND: Good night, my child.

YOUNG WIFE: Good night.

6
THE HUSBAND AND THE LITTLE MISS

(A private room in the Riedhof Restaurant; comfortable, unobtrusive elegance. On the table the remains of a meal: meringues with much whipped cream, fruit, cheese. White Hungarian wine in the glasses)

(HUSBAND smokes a Havana cigar, leans back on the corner of the table.)

(LITTLE MISS sits on a chair beside him, scoops the whipped cream out of a meringue and sucks it up.)

HUSBAND: It's good?

LITTLE MISS: *(Uninterruptible)* Mm!

HUSBAND: Like another?

LITTLE MISS: No, I've eaten too much already.

HUSBAND: You've no wine left.

(HUSBAND *fills up* LITTLE MISS's *glass.*)

LITTLE MISS: No...I'll only leave it, sir.

HUSBAND: Sir? Don't be so formal with me.

LITTLE MISS: Well, you're not so easy to get used to, sir.

HUSBAND: "Sir" again. Come and sit by me.

LITTLE MISS: One moment—I'm not through.

(HUSBAND *gets up, stands behind* LITTLE MISS's *chair and puts his arms round her, turning her head toward him.*)

LITTLE MISS: What is it now?

HUSBAND: I'd like to have a kiss.

LITTLE MISS: *(Gives him a kiss)* You're pretty fresh, you are.

HUSBAND: You only just noticed?

LITTLE MISS: Oh, I noticed before...in the street. You must have quite an opinion of me.

HUSBAND: How's that?

LITTLE MISS: Going straight to a private dining room with you.

HUSBAND: You didn't go "straight" to this private dining room.

LITTLE MISS: You've a nice way of asking.

HUSBAND: You think so?

LITTLE MISS: And after all, what's wrong about it?

HUSBAND: Precisely.

LITTLE MISS: Whether you take a walk or...

HUSBAND: It's much too cold for a walk, isn't it?

LITTLE MISS: Much too cold!

HUSBAND: But in here it's nice and warm, don't you think?

(HUSBAND *has sat down again and put his arm round* LITTLE MISS, *pulling her over to his side.*)

LITTLE MISS: *(Weakly)* Hey!

HUSBAND: Now tell me... You'd noticed me before, hadn't you?

LITTLE MISS: Sure. In the Singer Strasse.

HUSBAND: I don't mean today. The day before yesterday and the day before that. I was following you.

LITTLE MISS: There's plenty follow me!

HUSBAND: I can imagine. Did you notice me?

LITTLE MISS: Well...um...you know what happened to me the other day? My cousin's husband followed me in the dark, and didn't recognize me.

HUSBAND: Did he speak to you?

LITTLE MISS: The idea! You think everybody's as fresh as you?

HUSBAND: It happens.

LITTLE MISS: Sure it happens.

HUSBAND: Well, what do *you* do?

LITTLE MISS: Me? Nothing. I just don't answer.

HUSBAND: Hm...you answered me.

LITTLE MISS: Well, are you mad at me?

HUSBAND: *(Kisses her violently)* Your lips taste of whipped cream.

LITTLE MISS: Oh, they're sweet by nature.

HUSBAND: Many men have told you that, have they?

LITTLE MISS: Many men! The ideas you get!

HUSBAND: Be honest with me. How many men have kissed these lips?

LITTLE MISS: If I tell you, you won't believe me.

HUSBAND: Why not?

LITTLE MISS: Guess.

HUSBAND: Let's say—um—but you mustn't be angry!

LITTLE MISS: Why should I be?

HUSBAND: Well, at a guess...twenty.

LITTLE MISS: *(Breaking away from him)* Why not a hundred while you're at it?

HUSBAND: It was only a guess.

LITTLE MISS: It was a bad guess.

HUSBAND: Let's say—ten.

LITTLE MISS: *(Offended)* Oh sure. A girl who lets you talk to her in the street and goes straight to a private dining room!

HUSBAND: We're in a restaurant, the waiter can come in any time—nothing to it.

LITTLE MISS: That's just what I thought.

HUSBAND: Have you ever been in a private dining room before?

LITTLE MISS: Well, yes.

HUSBAND: I like that: you're honest.

LITTLE MISS: It wasn't like you think. I was with my girl friend and her fiancé during the last Carnival.

HUSBAND: Well, it wouldn't be a tragedy if you'd been—with your boyfriend.

LITTLE MISS: I haven't got a boyfriend.

HUSBAND: Go on!

LITTLE MISS: Cross my heart.

HUSBAND: You don't mean to tell me I...

LITTLE MISS: What? ...There hasn't been anyone—for more than six months.

HUSBAND: I see.... And before that? Who was it?

LITTLE MISS: What are you so inquisitive for?

HUSBAND: Because...I'm in love with you!

LITTLE MISS: Really?

HUSBAND: Hadn't you noticed? Come on, tell me.

(HUSBAND *pulls* LITTLE MISS *close to him.*)

LITTLE MISS: Tell you what?

HUSBAND: Who he was.

LITTLE MISS: *(Laughing)* Oh, a man.

HUSBAND: Come on, come on, who was he?

LITTLE MISS: He was a little bit like you.

HUSBAND: Indeed.

LITTLE MISS: If you hadn't been so much like him....

HUSBAND: So that's why you let me speak to you!

LITTLE MISS: Well, yes.

HUSBAND: I don't know whether to be glad or sorry.

LITTLE MISS: If I was you, I'd be glad.... The way you talk reminds me of him too...and the way you look at a girl...

HUSBAND: What was his name?

LITTLE MISS: Don't look at me like that, no, please!

(HUSBAND *takes* LITTLE MISS *in his arms. A long, hot kiss.*)

(LITTLE MISS *shakes herself free and tries to get up.*)

HUSBAND: What's the matter?

LITTLE MISS: Time to go.

HUSBAND: Later.

LITTLE MISS: No, I *must* go home. Really. What do you think mother will say?

HUSBAND: You live with your mother?

LITTLE MISS: What did you think?

HUSBAND: Just the two of you?

LITTLE MISS: The five of us. Two boys and three girls.

HUSBAND: Don't sit so far away. Are you the eldest?

LITTLE MISS: No. I'm the second. First there's Kathi, she goes out to work. In a flower shop. Then there's me.

HUSBAND: What do you do?

LITTLE MISS: Stay at home.

HUSBAND: All the time?

LITTLE MISS: Well, one of us has got to be home.

HUSBAND: And what do you tell your mother when you get home late?

LITTLE MISS: It doesn't often happen.

HUSBAND: Tonight for example. Your mother does ask you?

LITTLE MISS: Oh, sure. However careful I am when I get home, she wakes up every time.

HUSBAND: What will you tell her tonight?

LITTLE MISS: I guess I'll have been to the theater.

HUSBAND: Will she believe you?

LITTLE MISS: Why not? I often go to the theater. Only last Sunday I was at the Opera with my girlfriend and her fiancé—and my older brother.

HUSBAND: Where do you get the tickets?

LITTLE MISS: My brother's a barber.

HUSBAND: Of course, barbers... A theatrical barber?

LITTLE MISS: Why are you pumping me like this?

HUSBAND: I'm interested. And what's your other brother?

LITTLE MISS: He's still at school. Wants to be a teacher. Imagine!

HUSBAND: And you've a younger sister too?

LITTLE MISS: Yes, she's only a brat, but you've got to keep an eye on her. You've no idea what these girls learn at school. The other day I caught her on a date!

HUSBAND: What?

LITTLE MISS: I did. With a boy from the school opposite. She was out walking with him in the Strozzi Gasse at half-past seven!

HUSBAND: What did you do?

LITTLE MISS: Well, she got a spanking.

HUSBAND: You're as strict as that?

LITTLE MISS: There's no one else to do it. My older sister's in the shop, Mother does nothing but grumble— so everything falls on me.

HUSBAND: God, you're sweet! *(He kisses her and grows more tender.)* And you remind me of someone, too.

LITTLE MISS: Do I? Who is she?

HUSBAND: No one in particular...you remind me of the time when...well, my youth! Come, drink up, child!

LITTLE MISS: How old are you? ...Um...I don't even know your name.

HUSBAND: Karl.

LITTLE MISS: Honest? Your name's Karl?

HUSBAND: *He* was called Karl?

LITTLE MISS: Really, it's a miracle...it's too... No, those eyes! ...That look! *(She shakes her head.)*

HUSBAND: You still haven't told me who he was.

LITTLE MISS: A bad man, that 's what he was, or he wouldn't have dropped me.

HUSBAND: Did you like him a lot?

LITTLE MISS: Sure I liked him a lot.

HUSBAND: I know what he was: a lieutenant.

LITTLE MISS: No, he wasn't in the Army. They wouldn't take him. His father's got a house in...but why do you want to know?

HUSBAND: *(Kisses her)* Your eyes are gray really. I thought they were black.

LITTLE MISS: Well, aren't they nice enough for you?

(HUSBAND kisses LITTLE MISS's eyes.)

LITTLE MISS: Oh, no—I can't stand that—please, please.... Oh God! ...No, let me get up...

HUSBAND: *(Increasingly tender)* Oh, no! No!

LITTLE MISS: Karl, please!

HUSBAND: How old are you? Eighteen, is it?

LITTLE MISS: Nineteen now.

HUSBAND: Nineteen...and I...

LITTLE MISS: You're thirty....

HUSBAND: And...a little more...

LITTLE MISS: At that, he was thirty-two when I met him!

HUSBAND: How long ago?

LITTLE MISS: I can't remember.... You know what, there was something in the wine! Everything's turning round!

HUSBAND: Hold on to me. Like this...

(HUSBAND *pulls* LITTLE MISS *to him and becomes more and more tender; she scarcely defends herself.*)

HUSBAND: I'll tell you something, treasure, now we might really go.

LITTLE MISS: Yes—home.

HUSBAND: Not home exactly...

LITTLE MISS: What do you mean? ...Oh no, no! ...I wouldn't!

HUSBAND: Now, listen to me, my child, next time we meet, you know, we'll arrange it so... (*He has slipped to the floor, his head in her lap.*) That's good, oh, that's good!

LITTLE MISS: What are you doing? She kisses his hair. See, there must have been something in the wine...so sleepy... Hey, what happens if I can't get up? But...but look, Karl! ...If somebody comes in... Please...the waiter!

HUSBAND: No waiter'll...come in here...not in...your lifetime.

*****

(LITTLE MISS *leans back in a corner of the sofa, her eyes shut.*)

(HUSBAND *walks up and down the small room, after lighting a cigar. A longish silence*)

HUSBAND: (*Looks at* LITTLE MISS *for a long time, then says to himself*) Who knows what sort of person she really is—God in heaven! ...So quickly... Wasn't very careful of me... Hm...

LITTLE MISS: *(Without opening her eyes)* There must have been something in that wine.

HUSBAND: How's that?

LITTLE MISS: Otherwise...

HUSBAND: Why blame everything on the wine?

LITTLE MISS: Where are you? Why are you so far away? Come here.

*(*HUSBAND *goes to* LITTLE MISS, *sits down.)*

LITTLE MISS: Now, tell me if you really like me.

HUSBAND: But you *know....* *(Interrupting himself quickly)* Of course I do.

LITTLE MISS: You see...there *is*... Come on, tell me the truth, what was in that wine?

HUSBAND: You think I go around poisoning people?

LITTLE MISS: Listen, I'm not like that, cross my heart— if you believe that of me...

HUSBAND: I don't think anything bad of you. I just think you like me.

LITTLE MISS: Yes...

HUSBAND: After all, if two young people are alone together, and have supper—there doesn't have to be anything in the wine.

LITTLE MISS: Oh, I was just gabbing.

HUSBAND: But why?

LITTLE MISS: *(Somewhat defiantly)* Because I was ashamed!

HUSBAND: That's ridiculous! There's no reason for it. Especially since I remind you of your first lover.

LITTLE MISS: Yes.

HUSBAND: Your first.

LITTLE MISS: Oh sure...

HUSBAND: Now it would interest me to know who the others were.

LITTLE MISS: There weren't any.

HUSBAND: That can't be true.

LITTLE MISS: Please don't nag me!

HUSBAND: A cigarette?

LITTLE MISS: No, thank you.

HUSBAND: Do you know what time it is?

LITTLE MISS: What?

HUSBAND: Half-past eleven.

LITTLE MISS: Really?

HUSBAND: Well...what about your mother? Used to it, is she?

LITTLE MISS: You want to send me home already?

HUSBAND: But *you* wanted—

LITTLE MISS: Look, you're different now. What have I done to you?

HUSBAND: My dear child, what's wrong?

LITTLE MISS: It was...the look in your eyes, honest, cross my heart. But for that you could have gone down on your knees.... A lot of men have *begged* me to go to a private dining room with them!

HUSBAND: Well, would you like to...to come here again... soon? Or some other place?

LITTLE MISS: I don't know.

(Pause)

HUSBAND: All right—when? But first I must explain: I don't live in Vienna. I...just come here now and then. For a couple of days.

LITTLE MISS: Go on—you aren't Viennese?

HUSBAND: Well, yes, I'm Viennese, but I live...out of town.

LITTLE MISS: Where?

HUSBAND: Goodness, *that* doesn't matter, does it?

LITTLE MISS: Don't worry, I won't go there.

HUSBAND: You can go there as much as you want! I live in Graz.

LITTLE MISS: Really?

HUSBAND: Yes. What's so astonishing about that?

LITTLE MISS: You're married, aren't you?

HUSBAND: *(Greatly surprised)* Whatever makes you think so?

LITTLE MISS: It looks that way to me.

HUSBAND: And if I were, it wouldn't bother you any?

LITTLE MISS: Oh, I'd like it better if you were single. But you're married. I know.

HUSBAND: What makes you think so?

LITTLE MISS: Oh, if a man says he doesn't live in town and hasn't always got time...

HUSBAND: That isn't so unlikely, is it?

LITTLE MISS: I don't believe it.

HUSBAND: And it wouldn't give you a bad conscience to seduce a married man? Make him unfaithful?

LITTLE MISS: I bet your wife is no different.

HUSBAND: Whether I have a wife or not, such observations are beyond the pale! He has risen.

LITTLE MISS: What is it, Karl? Are you mad at me? Look, I didn't know you were married. Come on, let's be friends.

HUSBAND: *(Goes to her after a couple of seconds)* You really are strange creatures. *(At her side, he begins to caress her again.)* Oh, the female of the species!

LITTLE MISS: No...don't...and it's so late...

HUSBAND: Now listen to me. We must have a serious talk. I want to see you again—many times.

LITTLE MISS: Honest?

HUSBAND: But if so...I must be able to rely on you. I can't be watching all the time.

LITTLE MISS: Oh, I can look after myself.

HUSBAND: You're...well, not inexperienced exactly, but you're young, and—men in general are an unscrupulous bunch.

LITTLE MISS: And how!

HUSBAND: So, if you want to love me—only me— we'll be able to fix things up somehow, even if I do live in Graz. This place isn't right—someone could come in at any moment!

(LITTLE MISS snuggles up to HUSBAND.)

HUSBAND: Next time let's make it somewhere else, yes?

LITTLE MISS: Yes.

HUSBAND: Where we can't be disturbed.

LITTLE MISS: Right.

HUSBAND: *(Embraces her with fervor)* The rest we can talk over on the way home. *(He gets up, opens the door.)* Waiter...the check!

7
THE LITTLE MISS AND THE POET

(A small room, comfortably furnished, in good taste. Drapes leave it in semi-darkness. Red net curtains. A big desk littered with papers and books. Against the wall, an upright piano.)

(LITTLE MISS and POET enter together. POET locks the door.)

POET: Here we are, sweetheart.

(POET kisses LITTLE MISS.)

LITTLE MISS: *(In hat and cloak)* Oh, what a nice room! Only you can't see anything!

POET: Your eyes will have to get used to semi-darkness. Those sweet eyes!

(POET kisses LITTLE MISS's eyelids.)

LITTLE MISS: These sweet eyes won't have time to get used to it.

POET: How's that?

LITTLE MISS: Because I can't stay more than one minute.

POET: Do take your hat off.

LITTLE MISS: For one minute?

POET: *(Pulls out her hatpin, takes the hat, puts it on one side)* And your cloak.

LITTLE MISS: What are you up to? I've got to go!

POET: First you must rest. We've been walking three hours.

LITTLE MISS: We were in the carriage.

POET: Coming home, yes. But in Weidling-am-Bach we were three solid hours on foot. Now do sit down, child...wherever you like...at the desk.... No, that isn't comfortable. Sit on the sofa. Here. *(He puts her down on the sofa.)* If you're tired, you can stretch out. Like this.

(POET makes LITTLE MISS lie down.)

POET: With your little head on the cushion.

LITTLE MISS: *(Laughing)* But I'm not a bit tired.

POET: You *think* you aren't. And now if you feel sleepy, you can go to sleep. I'll keep perfectly quiet. Or I can play you a lullaby...one of my own. *(He goes to the piano.)*

LITTLE MISS: Your own?

POET: Yes.

LITTLE MISS: But, Robert, I thought you were a doctor.

POET: How's that? I told you I was a writer.

LITTLE MISS: Well, writers *are* doctors, aren't they?

POET: Of philosophy? Not all writers. Not me, for instance. Why did you bring *that* up?

LITTLE MISS: Because you said the piece you were going to play was your own.

POET: Oh well...maybe it isn't. It doesn't matter. It never matters who's done a thing—just so long as it's beautiful—you agree?

LITTLE MISS: Oh sure...as long as it's beautiful.

POET: Do you know what I meant by that?

LITTLE MISS: By what?

POET: What I said just now.

LITTLE MISS: *(Drowsily)* Oh, sure.

POET: *(Gets up, goes to her and strokes her hair)* You didn't understand a word.

LITTLE MISS: Now look, I 'm *not* stupid.

POET: Of course you are. That's why I love you. It's a fine thing for women to be stupid. In *your* way, that is.

LITTLE MISS: Hey, don't be rude!

POET: Little angel! Isn't it nice to just lie there on a soft Persian rug?

LITTLE MISS: Oh yes. But can't we have the light on?

POET: Oh no ... Today we were bathing in sunshine all day long. Now we've come out of the bath, so to speak, and we're wrapping the twilight round us like a bathrobe. *(He laughs.)* No, it'll have to be put a little differently...won't it?

LITTLE MISS: Will it?

POET: *(Edging away from her)* It's divine, this stupidity! *(He takes out a notebook and writes a few words in it. In an undertone)* Sun—bath—twilight—robe... *(He puts the notebook in his pocket, laughs.)* And now tell me, treasure, wouldn't you like something to eat or drink?

LITTLE MISS: I'm not thirsty. But I *am* hungry.

POET: Hm...now, I'd rather you were thirsty. The cognac's right here, but if it's food I'll have to go out and get it.

LITTLE MISS: Can't they bring it up for you?

POET: Never mind. I'll go. What would you like?

LITTLE MISS: It isn't worth it, I've got to go.

POET: I'll tell you what: when we leave, we'll go and have supper somewhere.

LITTLE MISS: I haven't the time. And—where could we go? We'd be seen.

POET: You know so many people?

LITTLE MISS: It's enough if *one* of them sees us.

POET: How so?

LITTLE MISS: What do you think? If Mother heard anything...

POET: We could go to a place where nobody *could* see us. There are restaurants with private rooms...

LITTLE MISS: *(Sings)* "Just to share a private dining room with you..."

POET: Ever been to a private dining room?

LITTLE MISS: As a matter of fact I have.

POET: Who was the lucky man?

LITTLE MISS: I was with my girl friend and her fiancé.

POET: I'm supposed to believe that?

LITTLE MISS: Suit yourself.

POET: *(Close to her)* Did you blush? It's so dark in here, I can't make out your features. *(He touches her cheek with his hand.)* Even so—I recognize you.

LITTLE MISS: Well, take care you don't mix me up with another girl.

POET: Peculiar! I can't remember what you look like.

LITTLE MISS: Thank you very much.

POET: *(Seriously)* Do you know, it's rather spooky—I can't visualize your face—in a certain sense I've *forgotten* you. Now, if I couldn't recognize your voice either...what would you be?

LITTLE MISS: What *are* you talking about?

POET: Nothing, angel, nothing. Where are your lips?

(POET kisses LITTLE MISS.)

LITTLE MISS: Won't you put the light on?

POET: No... *(He grows very tender.)* Tell me if you love me!

LITTLE MISS: Oh, I do. I do!

POET: But... *(He sighs.)*

LITTLE MISS: Well—*he* was my fiancé.

POET: I'd rather you didn't think of him.

LITTLE MISS: Oh...what are you doing...now look...

POET: Let's imagine we're in a castle in India!

LITTLE MISS: I'm sure no Indian could be as naughty as you.

POET: Divine! If only you had an inkling of what you mean to me...

LITTLE MISS: Well, what?

POET: Don't push me away all the time. I'm not doing anything—yet.

LITTLE MISS: Listen, my corset hurts.

POET: Take it off.

LITTLE MISS: But you mustn't be naughty. *(She rises and takes off her corset.)*

POET: Tell me, doesn't it interest you to know my last name?

LITTLE MISS: Oh, yes—what is it?

POET: I'd better not tell you my name. I'll tell you what I call myself.

LITTLE MISS: What's the difference?

POET: Well, what I call myself—as a writer.

LITTLE MISS: You don't write under your real name?

(POET, *close to her*)

LITTLE MISS: Ah...please! ...Don't!

POET: O the sweet odor that rises from you!

(POET *kisses* LITTLE MISS's *bosom.*)

LITTLE MISS: You're tearing my chemise.

POET: Off with it all! Away with these...superfluities!

LITTLE MISS: *Robert!*

POET: Let's enter our Indian castle!

LITTLE MISS: First tell me if you *really* love me.

POET: I worship you! (*He kisses her hotly.*) I *worship* you, my springtime...my...

LITTLE MISS: Robert... Robert...

*****

(POET *is dressing.* LITTLE MISS *is naked.*)

POET: That was bliss supernal.... I call myself...

LITTLE MISS: Robert. *My* Robert.

POET: I call myself Biebitz.

LITTLE MISS: Why do you call yourself Biebitz?

POET: You know the name?

LITTLE MISS: No.

POET: You don't know the name Biebitz? How divine! But you're pretending?

LITTLE MISS: Cross my heart, I've never heard it.

POET: You never go to the theatre?

LITTLE MISS: Oh, yes. Just the other day I got taken— by my girl friend's uncle—and my girl friend— and we went to the Opera—*Cavalleria Rusticana!*

POET: Hmm, but you don't go to the Burg Theater?

LITTLE MISS: Nobody ever gave me a ticket.

POET: I'll send you a ticket!

LITTLE MISS: Make it something funny.

POET: You wouldn't like something sad?

LITTLE MISS: Not as much.

POET: Even if it's by me?

LITTLE MISS: You write for the theatre?!

POET: Excuse me, I just want to light a candle. I haven't seen you since you became mine. Angel! *(He lights a candle.)*

LITTLE MISS: Hey, don't! I feel ashamed. Give me a blanket anyway!

POET: Later!

(POET walks up to LITTLE MISS with the light and contemplates her naked body.)

LITTLE MISS: *(Covers her face with her hands)* Robert!

POET: You're beautiful. You *are* Beauty! You are Nature herself perhaps! You are Sacred Simplicity!

LITTLE MISS: Ouch! You're dripping wax on me! Why can't you be more careful?

POET: *(Puts the candlestick down)* You're what I've been looking for all this time. You love me—just me—you'd love me the same if I were a shop assistant. It does me good. I'll confess that till now I couldn't get rid of a certain suspicion. Tell me, hadn't you the least idea I was Biebitz?

LITTLE MISS: I don't know any Biebitz.

POET: Such is fame! Never mind, forget what I told you, forget even the name I told you. I'm Robert for you, and I want to remain Robert. *(Gaily)* I'm not a writer at all, I'm a shop assistant. In the evenings I play the piano for folk singers!

LITTLE MISS: Now you have me all mixed up...and the way you look at a girl! What's eating you?

POET: It's strange—it's hardly ever happened to me, my treasure—I feel like crying. You've got under my skin. Let's stay together, hm? We're going to love one another very much.

LITTLE MISS: Listen, is that true about the folk singing?

POET: Yes, but don't ask any more. If you love me, don't ask. Tell me, could you make yourself quite free for a couple of weeks?

LITTLE MISS: What do you mean, quite free?

POET: Well, away from home.

LITTLE MISS: How could I? What would Mother say? Anyway, everything would go wrong at home without me.

POET: I'd been thinking how lovely it would be to live with you for a few weeks quite alone, somewhere, in distant solitude, in the depths of the forests! Thou Nature art my Goddess! And then, one day, farewell— to go who knows whither?

LITTLE MISS: Now you're talking of good-bye. And I thought you liked me.

POET: That's just it! *(He bends down and kisses her on the forehead.)* Sweet creature!

LITTLE MISS: Hold me tight, I'm cold.

POET: It's time to get dressed. Wait, I'll light some more candles.

LITTLE MISS: *(Gets up)* Don't look! *(She is getting dressed.)*

POET: No *(At the window)* Tell me, child, are you happy?

LITTLE MISS: How do you mean?

POET: In general I mean: are you happy?

LITTLE MISS: Things could be better.

POET: You've told me of the state of affairs at home, I know you aren't exactly a princess. I mean, setting all that aside, do you feel you're alive? Do you feel you are really alive?

LITTLE MISS: You got a comb? *(She is dressed now.)*

POET: *(Goes to the dressing-table, gives her the comb, contemplates her)* God, you're enchanting!

LITTLE MISS: No...don't!

POET: Come, stay with me a little longer, let me get something for our supper, and...

LITTLE MISS: But it's much too late.

POET: It's not nine yet.

LITTLE MISS: Oh well, but I've got to hurry.

POET: When shall we meet next?

LITTLE MISS: When would you like to see me?

POET: Tomorrow?

LITTLE MISS: What's tomorrow?

POET: Saturday.

LITTLE MISS: Oh, I can't make it. Got to see our guardian. With my little sister.

POET: Sunday, then... Look, I'm not Biebitz, Biebitz is a friend of mine. His play is on next Sunday. I'll send you a ticket, and come to the theatre to get you afterwards. You'll tell me how you liked the play, won't you?

LITTLE MISS: This Biebitz thing...well, I may be stupid but...

POET: When I know how you feel about the play, I'll really know *you.*

LITTLE MISS: I'm ready!

POET: Let's go, then, my treasure.

(LITTLE MISS *and* POET *leave.)*

8
THE POET AND THE ACTRESS

(A room in a country inn. It is an evening in spring; moonlight; the windows are open. All is still.)

(The POET *and the* ACTRESS *enter; as they come in, the flame of the candle which he is carrying goes out.)*

POET: Oh!

ACTRESS: What's the matter?

POET: The candle. But we don't need it. Look, it's quite light!

(The ACTRESS *sinks on her knees at the window, folding her hands.)*

POET: What's the matter with you?

ACTRESS: *(Indignant)* Can't you see I'm praying?

POET: You believe in God?

ACTRESS: What do you think I am—an anarchist? Kneel down beside me. You could use a prayer once in a while.

*(*POET *kneels and puts his arms round* ACTRESS.)*

ACTRESS: You lecher! *(She gets up.)* And do you know to whom I was praying?

POET: To God, I presume.

ACTRESS: *(With great scorn)* Oh yes? It was to you
I prayed.

POET: Then why look out of the window?

ACTRESS: Tell me where you've dragged me off to,
seducer.

POET: It was your idea, my child. You wanted to go
to the country. You wanted to come here.

ACTRESS: Well, wasn't I right?

POET: And only two hours from Vienna—perfect
solitude! What a landscape!

ACTRESS: You could write poetry here, if you had the
talent.

(Pause)

POET: Have you been here before?

ACTRESS: I lived here for years.

POET: With whom?

ACTRESS: Oh, with Fritz, of course.

POET: I see.

ACTRESS: I worshiped that man.

POET: You told me.

ACTRESS: Oh, I beg your pardon—I can leave if I bore
you.

POET: *You* bore me? ...You have no idea what you
mean to me... You're the Divine Spark, you're Genius...
You're Sacred Simplicity.... But you shouldn't talk
about Fritz—now.

ACTRESS: He was an aberration, yes... Oh well...

POET: It's good you see that.

ACTRESS: Come over and kiss me.

(POET *kisses* ACTRESS.)

ACTRESS: And now we're going to say good-night.

POET: What do you mean?

ACTRESS: I'm going to bed.

POET: But this "good-night" business...where am *I* going to sleep?

ACTRESS: I'm sure there are other rooms in this inn.

POET: For me the other rooms have singularly little attraction. By the way, I'd better light up, hadn't I?

ACTRESS: Yes.

POET: *(Lights the candle on the bedside table)* What a pretty room... Lined with pictures of the Saints! Folks 'round here are *really* religious. Wouldn't it be interesting to spend time with them! Get to know our fellow men!

ACTRESS: Stop talking bosh, and give me my pocketbook, will you, it's on the table.

POET: Here, my own!

(ACTRESS *takes from the pocket book a small framed picture and puts it on the bedside table.)*

POET: What's *that*?

ACTRESS: Our Lady.

POET: I beg your pardon?

ACTRESS: The Blessed Virgin.

POET: I see. You never travel without her?

ACTRESS: Never. That's my mascot. Now go, Robert.

POET: What sort of a joke is this? Don't you want me to help you?

ACTRESS: I want you to go.

POET: Will you ever take me back?

ACTRESS: Perhaps.

POET: When?

ACTRESS: Oh, in about ten minutes.

POET: *(Kisses her)* Darling! See you in ten minutes.

ACTRESS: Where will you be?

POET: I shall walk up and down under your window. I love to walk at night! I get my best ideas in the open air. Especially when you're near. Wafted by your longings, floating on your art...

ACTRESS: You talk like an idiot.

POET: *(Sorrowfully)* Some might have said—like a poet.

ACTRESS: Now go. And don't start anything with the waitress.

(The POET departs.)

(ACTRESS undresses. She listens to the POET going down the wooden stairs and then to his steps beneath the open window. As soon as she is naked, she goes to the window, looks down, sees him standing there, calls to him in a whisper.)

ACTRESS: Come!

(The POET comes up in a hurry; rushes toward ACTRESS. In the meantime she has gone to bed and put out the light. He locks the door.)

ACTRESS: Well, now you may sit down and tell me a story.

POET: *(Sits by her on the bed)* A story?

ACTRESS: Tell me—who are you being unfaithful to— at this moment?

POET: I'm not being unfaithful—at this moment.

ACTRESS: Don't worry, I'm unfaithful too!

POET: I can imagine.

ACTRESS: And who do you think it is?

POET: My dear child, I wouldn't have a notion.

ACTRESS: Guess, then.

POET: Wait a moment... Well, your producer?

ACTRESS: My dear, I'm not a chorus girl.

POET: Just an idea.

ACTRESS: Guess again.

POET: Your leading man—Benno.

ACTRESS: Pooh, that man doesn't like women, didn't you know? He's having an affair with the postman. Kiss me.

(POET *embraces* ACTRESS.)

ACTRESS: I have a suggestion. Get in bed with me.

POET: I accept (*He starts to undress.*)

ACTRESS: Quick.

POET: Well...if *I'd* had my way, I'd have been... Listen!

ACTRESS: What?

POET: The crickets are chirping outside.

ACTRESS: You must be mad, my dear, there are no crickets in these parts.

POET: But you can hear them! (*He is now naked.*)

ACTRESS: Get into bed.

POET: *Me voici.*

(POET *gets in bed with* ACTRESS.)

ACTRESS: And now lie still... Uh! ...Don't move!

POET: What's the idea?

ACTRESS: I suppose you'd like to have an affair with me.

POET: I thought you might realize that sooner or later.

ACTRESS: A lot of men would like an affair with me.

POET: But at this particular moment the odds are rather strongly in my favor.

ACTRESS: Come, my cricket. From now on I'm going to call you Cricket...

POET: Fine...

ACTRESS: Now—who am I deceiving?

POET: Huh? Me, maybe.

ACTRESS: My child, you should have your head examined.

POET: Or maybe someone...you've never seen...someone you don't know... He's meant for you, but you can never find him...

ACTRESS: Cricket, don't talk such fantastic rot!

POET: ...Isn't it strange...even you...and one would have liked to believe— But no, it would just be...spoiling all that's best about you if one... Come, come...come!

*****

ACTRESS: That's better than acting in damn silly plays. You agree?

(ACTRESS and POET are sitting up in bed.)

POET: Well, I think it's as well you have a part in a reasonable play.

ACTRESS: Meaning yours, you conceited pup.

POET: Of course.

ACTRESS: (Seriously) It really is a wonderful play

POET: You see!

ACTRESS: You're a genius!

POET: By the way, why did you cancel your performance two nights ago? There was nothing wrong with you.

ACTRESS: I wanted to annoy you.

POET: Why?

ACTRESS: You're so conceited. Everybody says so.

POET: Really.

ACTRESS: But I told them: that man has a *right* to be conceited.

POET: And what did they say to that?

ACTRESS: What would they say? I never speak to them.

POET: I see.

ACTRESS: They'd like to poison me. *(Pause)* But they won't succeed.

POET: Don't think of them. Just be happy we're here, and tell me you love me.

ACTRESS: You need further proof?

POET: Oh, that kind of thing can't be *proved.*

ACTRESS: This is just lovely! What more do you want?

POET: How many others did you try to prove it to this way? And did you love them all?

ACTRESS: Oh, no. I loved only one.

POET: *(Embracing her)* My...

ACTRESS: Fritz.

POET: My name is Robert. What am I to you, if it's Fritz you're thinking of?

ACTRESS: A whim.

POET: Nice to know!

ACTRESS: Tell me, aren't you proud?

POET: Why should I be proud?

ACTRESS: I think you have some reason.

POET: Oh, because of that!

ACTRESS: Yes, because of that, my pale cricket. How about the chirping? Are they still chirping?

POET: All the time. Can't you hear?

ACTRESS: I can hear. But that's frogs, my child.

POET: You're wrong: frogs croak.

ACTRESS: Certainly, they croak.

POET: But not here, my dear child. This is chirping.

ACTRESS: You're the most pigheaded creature I've ever come across. Kiss me, frog.

POET: Please don't call me that. It makes me nervous.

ACTRESS: What do you want me to call you?

POET: I've got a name: Robert.

ACTRESS: Oh, that's too dull.

POET: Call me simply by my name!

ACTRESS: All right, Robert, kiss me... Ah! (*She kisses him.*) Are you content now, frog? Ha, ha, ha!

POET: May I light a cigarette?

ACTRESS: Give me one.

(POET *takes the cigarette case from the bedside table, takes out two, lights both and hands one to* ACTRESS.)

ACTRESS: By the way, you never said a word about my work last night.

POET: What work?

ACTRESS: Well...!

POET: Oh, I see. I wasn't at the theatre.

ACTRESS: I guess you like your little joke.

POET: Not at all. When you cancelled your performance the day before yesterday, I assumed you couldn't be in full possession of your powers yesterday. So I didn't go.

ACTRESS: You missed something.

POET: Indeed?

ACTRESS: I was sensational. People turned pale.

POET: You could see them?

ACTRESS: Benno said to me "You were a goddess, darling."

POET: Hm...and so sick one day earlier.

ACTRESS: Yes. And do you know why? Out of longing for you.

POET: You just told me you canceled the performance to annoy me!

ACTRESS: What do you know of my love for you? That sort of thing leaves you cold. I was in a fever for nights on end. With a temperature of a hundred and five.

POET: A high temperature just for a whim!

ACTRESS: A whim, you call it? I die for love of you, and you call it a whim?

POET: What about Fritz?

ACTRESS: What about him? What about him? I've heard too much about that ... that cheap crook!

(ACTRESS *and* POET *are both still in bed.*)

9
THE ACTRESS AND THE COUNT

(The ACTRESS'*s bedroom, luxuriously furnished. It is noon; the blinds are still down; on the bedside table, a burning candle; she is lying in her four-poster in rather lavish night attire. Numerous newspapers are strewn about on the covers.)*

(The COUNT *enters, in the uniform of a captain of Dragoons. He stops at the door.)*

ACTRESS: It's you, Count!

COUNT: Your good mother gave me permission, or of course I wouldn't...

ACTRESS: Please come right in.

COUNT: I kiss your hand. A thousand pardons—coming straight in from the street—you know, I can't see a thing. Yes...here we are. *(Near the bed)* I kiss your hand.

ACTRESS: Sit down, my dear Count. *(He takes a chair not too close to the bed.)*

COUNT: Your mother said you weren't very well, *Fräulein.* Nothing too serious, I hope?

ACTRESS: Nothing serious? I was dying!

COUNT: Oh dear me! Not really?

ACTRESS: In any case it's kind of you to...trouble to call.

COUNT: Dying! And only last night you played like a goddess!

ACTRESS: It was a triumph, I believe.

COUNT: Colossal! People were absolutely knocked out. As for myself, well...

ACTRESS: Thanks for the lovely flowers! *(Turns her eyes towards a large basket of flowers on a small table by the window)*

COUNT: Last night you were positively *strewn* with flowers and garlands!

ACTRESS: I left them all in my dressing room. Your basket was the only thing I brought home.

COUNT: *(Kisses her hand)* You're very kind.

(ACTRESS suddenly takes COUNT's hand and kisses it.)

COUNT: *Fräulein!*

ACTRESS: Don't be afraid, Count. It commits you to nothing!

COUNT: You're a strange creature...a puzzle, one might almost say.

ACTRESS: Fräulein Birken is...easier to solve?

COUNT: Oh, little Birken is no puzzle. Though... I know her only superficially.

ACTRESS: Indeed?

COUNT: Oh, believe me. But *you* are a problem. And that's what I want. Last night I realized what a great pleasure I'd been missing. It was the first time I've seen you act.

ACTRESS: Is that true?

COUNT: Oh, yes. You see, *Fräulein*, the theatre is also a problem. By the time I get there, the best part of the play'd be over, wouldn't it?

ACTRESS: You'll have to dine earlier from now on.

COUNT: I'd thought of that. Or of not dining at all. There's not much pleasure in it, is there—dining?

ACTRESS: What do you still find pleasure in, young fogey?

COUNT: I sometimes ask myself. Lulu says I'm a philosopher. What he means is: I think too much.

ACTRESS: Lulu?

COUNT: Friend of mine.

ACTRESS: It is a misfortune, all that thinking.

COUNT: I've time on my hands, so I think. You see, *Fräulein*, when they transferred me to Vienna, I thought it would be better. It'd be amusing, stimulating, the city. But it's much the same as up there.

ACTRESS: And where is "up there"?

COUNT: Well, down there, *Fräulein*, in Hungary. The small towns I used to be stationed in.

ACTRESS: What were you doing in Hungary?

COUNT: I'm telling you, dear lady—the Army.

ACTRESS: Enough to drive anyone mad, I should think!

COUNT: Oh, I don't know. In a way you have more to do than here: training recruits, exercising horses... It's really rather lovely, the big plain there. Such a sunset! Pity I'm not a painter! Often thought I'd paint one, if I were a painter. Why I tell you this boring stuff I don't know, *Fräulein*.

ACTRESS: Please, Count! I'm highly amused!

COUNT: You know, *Fräulein*, it's so easy to talk to you. Lulu told me it would be. It's a thing one doesn't often meet.

ACTRESS: In darkest Hungary!

COUNT: Or in Vienna! People are the same everywhere. Tell me, *Fräulein*, do you like people, really?

ACTRESS: Like them? I hate them! I don't want to see them. I never do see them. I'm always alone. This house is deserted!

COUNT: Just as I imagined: You're a misanthrope. It's bound to happen with artists. Moving in that more exalted sphere... Well, at least you know why you're alive.

ACTRESS: I haven't the remotest idea why I'm alive!

COUNT: Not really, *Fräulein*...famous...celebrated...

ACTRESS: Is that—happiness?

COUNT: Happiness doesn't exist. None of the things people chatter about really exist... Love, for instance.

ACTRESS: You may be right there.

COUNT: Enjoyment...intoxication...there's nothing wrong with them, they're real. But as soon as you don't—I don't quite know how to say it—as soon as you stop living for the present moment, as soon as you think of later on or earlier on... Well, the whole thing collapses. Don't you think so?

ACTRESS: *(Nods, her eyes very wide open)* You pluck out the heart of the mystery, my dear Count

COUNT: And you see, *Fräulein*, once you're clear about that, it doesn't matter if you live in Vienna or on the Hungarian plains or in the tiny town of Steinamanger. For example...where can I put my cap? ...Oh, thanks. Where were we?

ACTRESS: In the tiny town of Steinamanger.

COUNT: Whether I spend the evening at the Casino or the Club is all one.

ACTRESS: How does this tie in with love?

COUNT: If a man believes in love, there'll always be a girl to "love" him.

ACTRESS: Fräulein Birken, for example.

COUNT: Honestly, dear lady, I can't understand why you keep mentioning little Birken.

ACTRESS: She's your mistress, that's why.

COUNT: Who says so?

ACTRESS: Everyone.

COUNT: Except me.

ACTRESS: You fought a duel on her behalf!

COUNT: Possibly I was shot dead and didn't notice!

ACTRESS: Count, you are a man of honor. Sit a little closer.

COUNT: If I may. *(He moves his chair closer.)*

ACTRESS: Here. *(She draws him closer, and runs her fingers through his hair.)* I knew you would come today.

COUNT: Really?

ACTRESS: I knew it last night. In the theater.

COUNT: Oh, could you see me from the stage?

ACTRESS: My dear man, didn't you realize I was playing for you alone?

COUNT: How could that be?

ACTRESS: After I saw you in the front row, I was walking on air.

COUNT: I'd no idea you'd noticed me.

ACTRESS: Oh, you can drive a woman crazy with that dignity of yours!

COUNT: *Fräulein!*

ACTRESS: *"Fräulein"*? At least take your saber off!

COUNT: Permit me. *(He unbuckles his belt, leans the saber against the bed.)*

ACTRESS: And now kiss me!

(COUNT kisses ACTRESS. She does not let him go.)

ACTRESS: I wish I'd never set eyes on you.

COUNT: No, no, it's better so.

ACTRESS: Count, you're a *poseur*.

COUNT: A *poseur*?

ACTRESS: Many a man'd be happy to be in your shoes right now.

COUNT: *I'm* happy.

ACTRESS: Oh—I thought happiness didn't exist! Why do you look at me like that?

COUNT: I told you, *Fräulein*, you're a problem.

ACTRESS: Oh, bother philosophy! Ask me for something. You can have whatever you like.

COUNT: Well, then I beg leave *(Kisses her hand)* to return tonight.

ACTRESS: But I'm playing tonight.

COUNT: After the theater.

ACTRESS: Nothing else?

COUNT: Everything else. After the theater.

ACTRESS: *(Offended)* Then you can ask, you wretched *poseur*.

COUNT: You see, *Fräulein*...you see, my dear... We've been frank with each other till now. I'd find it all much nicer in the evening, after the theater...so much more comfortable.... At present, I've the feeling the door's going to open at any moment.

ACTRESS: This door doesn't open from the outside.

COUNT: *Fräulein*, wouldn't it be frivolous to spoil something at the start? When it might turn out to be beautiful?

ACTRESS: *Might* turn out!

COUNT: And to tell the truth, I find love in the morning pretty frightful.

ACTRESS: You're the craziest man I've ever come across.

COUNT: Women like you, *Fräulein*—no, you can call me a fool, but women like you... Well, one shouldn't have them before breakfast, that's all.

ACTRESS: God, you're sweet!

COUNT: You see I'm right, don't you? What I have in mind...

ACTRESS: Tell me what you have in mind.

COUNT: I'll wait for you after the theatre in my carriage, then we can drive off somewhere, well, and have supper and...

ACTRESS: I am not Fräulein Birken!

COUNT: One must be in the mood! I get in the mood at supper. It's lovely to drive home after supper, and then...

ACTRESS: And then?

COUNT: Let events take their natural course.

ACTRESS: Come closer. Closer!

COUNT: *(Sits down on the bed)* I must say, the perfume that comes from these pillows—*mignonette*, is it?

ACTRESS: It's hot in here, don't you think?

(COUNT bends down and kisses ACTRESS's throat.)

ACTRESS: Oh my dear Count, this isn't on your program.

COUNT: I have no program.

(ACTRESS *draws* COUNT *to her.*)

COUNT: It is hot.

ACTRESS: You find it so? And dark, like evening...
(*Pulling him to her.*) It is evening, Count. It's night....
Shut your eyes if it's too light for you. Come!

(COUNT *no longer defends himself.*)

*****

ACTRESS: What's that about being in the mood,
you *poseur*?

COUNT: *(Who is getting dressed)* You're a little devil.

ACTRESS: Count!

COUNT: All right, a little angel.

ACTRESS: And you should have been an actor. Really!
You understand women. Do you know what I'm going
to do now?

COUNT: Well?

ACTRESS: I'm going to tell you I never want to see you
again.

COUNT: Why?

ACTRESS: You're too dangerous. You turn a woman's
head. And now you stand there as if nothing has
happened.

COUNT: But...

ACTRESS: Remember, my dear Count, that I've just been
your mistress.

COUNT: Can I ever forget?

ACTRESS: So how about tonight?

COUNT: What do you mean?

ACTRESS: You intended to meet me after the theater?

COUNT: Oh, yes, all right: let's say the day after tomorrow.

ACTRESS: We were talking of tonight.

COUNT: There wouldn't be much sense in that.

ACTRESS: Fogey!

COUNT: I mean—how should I say—from the spiritual viewpoint.

ACTRESS: It's not your spirit that interests me!

COUNT: I don't believe body and spirit can be kept apart.

ACTRESS: Don't throw philosophy at me. When I want that, I read books.

COUNT: We never learn from books.

ACTRESS: That's why you'll be here tonight. We'll come to an agreement about the spiritual viewpoint, you...spiritualist!

COUNT: Then—with your permission—I'll wait in my carriage.

ACTRESS: You'll wait here. In my apartment.

COUNT: After the theatre?

ACTRESS: Of course.

(COUNT *buckles on his saber.*)

COUNT: And now it's time for me to go, *Fräulein*. I've been staying rather long as it is, for a formal visit.

ACTRESS: Well, it won't be a formal visit tonight!

COUNT: No?

ACTRESS: Give me one more kiss, little philosopher. Here, you seducer...you...sweet thing, you spiritualist, you...you polecat, you... *(After several emphatic kisses she emphatically pushes him away.)* My dear Count, it was a great honor.

COUNT: I kiss your hand, Fräulein. *(At the door) Au revoir! (He leaves.)*

ACTRESS: *Adieu*, tiny town of Steinamanger!

10
THE COUNT AND THE WHORE

(Morning, toward six o'clock. A mean little room: dirty yellow blinds are down; frayed green curtains. A chest of drawers, with a few photographs on it and a cheap lady's hat in conspicuously bad taste. On the table stands a kerosene lamp, still feebly alight; next to the lamp, a jug and a half empty glass. On the floor by the bed, untidy feminine clothing.)

*(*WHORE *is asleep in the bed, breathing evenly. On the sofa lies the* COUNT, *fully dressed and in a light overcoat; his hat is on the floor.)*

COUNT: *(Moves, rubs his eyes, rises with a start and, in a sitting position, looks round)* So I did go home with that female.... *(He jumps up, sees her bed.)* And here she is. To think what can happen to a man of my age! I don't remember a thing—did they carry me up? Drunk? ...I remember going into that whores' café with Lulu and... Silly to rack my brains. I'll be on my way. *(He looks at the sleeping girl.)* She sleeps soundly. I can't remember anything specific, but I'll put the money on her bedside table-and good-bye.... I've known a lot of girls who didn't look so virtuous... Lulu would say I'm philosophizing, but sleep does make us all equal, like his big brother—Death.... Hmm, I'd like to know if... No, I'd remember after all... No, no, I dropped down on the sofa right away...and *nothing* happened. *(He goes to the door.)* ...Oh, there's that. *(He takes out his wallet and is about to get a bill.)*

WHORE: *(Wakes up)* Um... Who's here so early? *(Recognizing him)* Hiya!

COUNT: Good morning. Slept well?

WHORE: *(Stretches)* Come here. Little kiss.

COUNT: *(Bends down, thinks better of it, pulls up short)* I was just going...

WHORE: Going?

COUNT: It's time, really.

WHORE: You want to go like this?

COUNT: *(Almost embarrassed)* Well...

WHORE: So long, then. Come back and see us.

COUNT: Yes. Good-bye. Don't you want to shake hands?

(WHORE pulls her hand from under the blanket and offers it.)

COUNT: *(Takes her hand, mechanically kisses it, catches himself, and laughs)* As if she were a princess!

WHORE: Why do you look at me like that?

COUNT: One could imagine all sorts of things if the place didn't reek of kerosene....

WHORE: Yes, that lamp's a pest.

COUNT: How old are you, actually?

WHORE: Well, what do you think?

COUNT: Twenty-four.

WHORE: Oh, sure!

COUNT: Older?

WHORE: Nineteen.

COUNT: And how long have you been...

WHORE: In the business? A year.

COUNT: You started early.

WHORE: Better too early than too late.

COUNT: *(Sits down on the bed)* Tell me, are you happy?

WHORE: What?

COUNT: Well, I mean—how's it going?

WHORE: I'm doing all right.

COUNT: I see.... Did it ever occur to you to do something different?

WHORE: What could I do?

COUNT: Well...you're a pretty girl, you could have a lover.

WHORE: Think I don't?

COUNT: But I mean, *one*, you know: one lover—who keeps you, so you don't have to go with just any man.

WHORE: I *don't* go with just any man. I can afford to be choosy, thank goodness.

(COUNT looks round the room.)

WHORE: *(Notices this)* Next month we're moving into town. The Spiegel Gasse.

COUNT: We?

WHORE: The madam and a couple of the girls.

COUNT: There are other girls here?

WHORE: In the next room...can't you hear? That's Milli, she was at the café too.

COUNT: Somebody's snoring.

WHORE: That's Milli all right! She'll snore till ten at night, then get up and go to the café.

COUNT: But that's an appalling life!

WHORE: You said it. And the madam gets fed up with her. I'm on the streets by twelve noon.

COUNT: I see... *(He gets up, again takes out his wallet, and puts a bill on her bedside table.)* Good-bye.

WHORE: Already? ...Come again soon. *(She turns over on her side.)*

COUNT: *(Stops again)* Tell me something. It doesn't mean a thing to you now?

WHORE: What?

COUNT: I mean, you don't have fun with it any more?

WHORE: *(Yawns)* I'm sleepy.

COUNT: It's all the same to you if a man is young or old, or if he...

WHORE: What are you asking all this for?

COUNT: Well... Upon my soul, now I know who you remind me of, it's...

WHORE: I look like somebody?

COUNT: Incredible, now, please don't say a word for at least a minute.... *(He stares at her.)* Exactly the same face, exactly the same face.

(COUNT suddenly kisses WHORE on the eyes.)

WHORE: Hey!

COUNT: It's a pity you aren't...something else...you could make your fortune.

WHORE: You're like Franz.

COUNT: Who's Franz?

WHORE: The waiter at the café.

COUNT: How am I just like him?

WHORE: He says I could make my fortune. And I should marry him.

COUNT: Why don't you?

WHORE: I don't want no marriage. Maybe later.

COUNT: Exactly the same eyes... Lulu'd certainly say I'm a fool—but I'm going to kiss your eyes once more. *(He does so.)* And now good-bye.

WHORE: So long.

COUNT: *(Turning at the door)* Listen...tell me...aren't you a little bit surprised?

WHORE: Why?

COUNT: That I want nothing from you.

WHORE: There's a lot of men don't feel like it in the morning.

COUNT: Well, yes... Listen, I'll come again soon!

WHORE: *(With closed eyes)* Good.

COUNT: When are you in?

WHORE: I'm always in. Ask for Leocadia.

COUNT: Leocadia ... Right. Well, good-bye. *(At the door)* I spend the night with one of these...and all I do is kiss her eyes because she reminds me of someone.... *(He turns to her.)* Tell me, Leocadia, does it often happen that a man goes away like this?

WHORE: In the morning?

COUNT: No...I mean, hasn't it occasionally happened that a man was with you—and didn't want anything?

WHORE: No. Never!

COUNT: What's the matter? Do you think I don't like you?

WHORE: Last night you liked me all right.

COUNT: I like you now.

WHORE: Last night you liked me better.

COUNT: Didn't I drop down on the sofa right away?

WHORE: Sure you did—with me.

COUNT: With you?

WHORE: But you went right off to sleep after.

COUNT: So that's how it was!

WHORE: You must've been good and drunk if you can't remember.

COUNT: I see.... All the same, there *is* a resemblance.... Good-bye... *(He listens.)* What's that?

WHORE: The chambermaid's started work. Give her something as you go out. The front door's open now, so you save on the janitor.

COUNT: Right. *(In the entrance hall)* So...it would have been beautiful if I'd only kissed her eyes. It would almost have been an adventure.... *(Calls out)* Good night!

WHORE: *(Calling back)* Good *morning*!

COUNT: Oh, yes. *(Calling back to her)* Good morning!

END OF PLAY

The New York Times, Tuesday, January 19, 1954

High Court Upsets Censors Of Films in New York, Ohio

Finds Objections Too Vague on 'La Ronde' and 'M'— No General Rule Made, but 2 Justices Oppose Any Restraints

by Luther A Huston

Washington, Jan 19—The Supreme court rules unanimously today that New York State could not censor as immoral the French file "La Ronde," which depicts amorous adventures in old Vienna....

The high court did not rule, however, as it had been asked to do when the cases were argued on Jan. 6 and 7, that all censorship of motion pictures prior to public exhibition was unconstitutional.

No written opinion was handed down. But the basis of the courts ruling appeared to be that the laws under which New York and Ohio had refused licenses to show the films did not provide definite standards on what constituted an "immoral" picture....

The members of the court had witnessed private showings of the pictures before hearing oral arguments.

The court relied, in its ruling on "La Ronde"...upon its decision in "The Miracle" case in 1952. New York had censored that picture on the ground that it was "sacrilegious."

In its finding that that case, the Supreme Court called
the word "sacrilegious" as embodied in the New York
Education Law too vague and indefinite to provide a
satisfactory standard for determining what constituted
sacrilege.

In "The Miracle" case, however, the tribunal declared
that motion pictures were "within the free speech
and free press guaranty of the First and Fourteenth
Amendments." These amendments forbid Congress
to make laws that might abridge press and speech
freedoms and forbid the states to abridge the privileges
or immunities of citizens of the United States.

It was under these sections of the Constitution that
Mrs Florence Perlow Shientag, counsel for the
Commercial Pictures Corporation in the "La Ronde"
case...asked for the court to outlaw all prior censorship
of movies.

Two justices today—William O Douglas and Hugo
L Black—apparently leaned in this direction. Although
they joined in the brief ruling that reversed New York
and Ohio state court decisions upholding the
censorship of "La Ronde" and "M", Justices Douglas
and Black felt that it did not go far enough. They would
have forbidden any censorship of motion pictures.

"The argument of Ohio and New York that the
Government may establish censorship over moving
pictures is one that I cannot accept," Justice Douglas
wrote in a concurring opinion shared by Justice Black.
"The First and Fourteenth Amendments say that
Congress and the states shall make 'no law' that
abridges freedom of speech or of the press.

"In order to sanction a system of censorship I would
have to saw that 'no law' does not mean what it says,
that 'no law' has to be qualified to mean 'some' laws.
I cannot take that step.

"In this nation every writer, actor, producer, no matter what medium of expression he may use, should be freed from the censor."

The fact that the seven other justices did not go as far as Justices Black and Douglas would have liked was attributed by lawyer to judicial reluctance to establish absolute rules.

These justices might have felt, it was said, that the court should not strike down every law under which state governments might prohibit the showing of pictures that were patently obscene or otherwise not in the public interest.

Censor Expected to Be Wary

Nonetheless, lawyers who argued the case said that today's ruling meant the "death knell" of state censorship on such grounds as immorality.... State censors, they contended, will now be extremely wary of refusing licenses on those grounds.

Pictures that might be declared obscene would hardly be submitted to the censors anyway, these attorneys felt, so there now remain very few grounds upon which boards of censorship may ban movies from public exhibition.

The Board of Regents of the University of the State of New York refused a license for "La Ronde" on April 4, 1951. The picture had been produced in France in 1950. The Commercial Pictures Corporation holds the American distribution rights, and the film has been show in more than 100 cities throughout this country.

On May 28 last year, the New York Court of Appeals upheld the right of the Regents to ban "La Ronde." Commercial Pictures appealed this ruling to the Supreme Court.

Mrs Shientag, who fought the case to the high court, argued that New York law never had been intended "to permit censorship of a theme." The "theme" of "La Ronde" was illicit love, but Mrs Shientag contended that the subject was so treated that it did not offend reasonable standards of public morality.

Although the name of Nathaniel L Goldstein, the State Attorney General, appeared on the brief for the Board of Regents, the case was argued in the high court by Charles A Brind Jr, counsel for the State Education Department.

Mr Brind contended that the New York law was in accord with the Federal Constitution and that the state had a right under is police powers, to ban a movie whose them from beginning to end was "promiscuity and seduction."....

www.ingramcontent.com/pod-product-compliance
Lightning Source LLC
Chambersburg PA
CBHW052157090426
42741CB00010B/2301